A Larger Christian Life

A Larger Christian Life

By

A.B. SIMPSON

CHRISTIAN PUBLICATIONS, INC.
Harrisburg, Pa.

Christian Publications, Inc.
Harrisburg, PA

Mass Market Edition
Assigned 1979 to
Horizon House Publishers

ISBN 0-88965-034-9

Printed in the United States of America

CONTENTS

I

The Possibilities of Faith

"If thou canst believe, all things are possible to him that believeth" [Mark 9:23].

THESE are bold and stupendous words. They open the treasure house of the Eternal King to sinful worms, and offer to the children of clay the privilege of God's own omnipotence and all the possibilities of His infinite resources. Side by side these two astounding declarations stand, *"All things are possible with God"; "All things are possible to him that believeth."*

I. Let us consider the possibilities of faith:—

1. Salvation is possible to him that believeth. No matter how vile the sin, how many or how great the sins, how aggravated the guilt, how deep the corruption, how long the career of impenitence and crime, it is everywhere and forever true, "He that believeth on the Son hath everlasting life," "Believe on the Lord Jesus and thou shalt be saved." And thus alone can any soul be saved, for it is just as true forever, no matter what qualifications the soul may possess, whether the highest morality or the deepest depravity, "He that believeth not shall be damned." This blessed text opens the gates of Paradise and all the possibilities of grace to any and every sinner, and "whosoever will, may come, and take the Water of Life freely."

2. Sanctification is possible to him that believeth. "Inheritance among them that are sanctified by faith that is in me," is still the inscription over the gates of our full inheritance. "Purifying our hearts by faith" is still the Divine process of full salvation. Thus alone can the soul be sanctified. It is not a work, but a gift of grace, and all grace must be by faith. It is not possible by

painful struggling; it is not possible by penance and self-torture; it is not possible by sickness, suffering or self-crucifixion; it is not possible by moral suasion, careful training, correct teaching and perfect example; it is not possible even by the dark, cold waters of death itself. The soul that dies unsanctified shall be unsanctified forever. "He that is holy, let him be holy still: he that is filthy, let him be filthy still." But it is possible to him that believeth. It is the gift of Jesus Christ; it is the incoming and indwelling of Jesus Christ; it is the interior life and divine imparting of the Holy Ghost, and it must be by faith alone. And it is possible to any soul that will believe, no matter how unholy it has been, no matter how perverse it is; as mean perhaps and crooked as Jacob, as gross as David in his darkest sin, as self-confident as Simon Peter, as willful and self-righteous as Paul—it may be and shall be made as spotless as the Son of God, as holy as the holiness of Jesus Himself, who comes to dwell within, if we will only believe and receive.

3. Divine healing is possible to him that believeth. "The prayer of faith shall save the sick," is still the Master's unaltered word for His suffering church. And this faith must be the faith of the receiver, for in the epistle it is said, "Let not him that wavereth think that he shall receive anything of the Lord." Still it is as true as when the Master touched the eyes of the blind men to whom He said it, "According to your faith be it unto you." It matters not how serious the disease, it may be as helpless as the cripple's who could not in any wise lift himself up; as chronic as the impotent man who lay for thirty and eight years helpless at the pool; as obscure and as despised a case as the poor blind men who begged by the wayside and whom the multitude thought unworthy of Christ's attention, or as the sinful woman of Syro-Phœnicia, to whom, as to others, the

healing came when He could say, "Great is thy faith: be it unto thee even as thou wilt." It is not the faith which heals, it is the God that the faith touches; but there is no other way of touching God except by faith, and therefore if we would receive His Almighty touch, we must believe.

4. All power for service is possible to him that believeth. The gift of the Holy Ghost is received by faith. The power of the apostles was in proportion to their faith. Shephen "full of faith and power" could meet all the wisdom of Saul of Tarsus and the synagogue of the Cilicians. The simple story of Barnabas is that "he was a good man, and full of the Holy Ghost and of faith and much people was added unto the Lord." The secret of effective preaching is not logic, or rhetoric, or elocution, but to be able to say, "I believed and therefore have I spoken." The success of some evangelists and Christian workers is out of all proportion to their talent or capacity in any direction, but they have one gift which they faithfully exercise and that is expecting God to give them souls; and therefore they are never disappointed. The church has yet to see in the present generation, the full possibilities of faith in the work of the Lord. The examples of a Moody and a Harrison are but types of what is possible for the humblest worker who with an eye single to the glory of God and simple fidelity to the gospel of Christ will dare to expect the mightiest results. Both these examples, perhaps the most marked instances of wide fruitfulness in the present generation, are persons without great natural gifts or educational advantages and therefore the more encouraging as incentives to the work of faith. Humble toiler in the vineyard of the Lord, will you go forth to all the possibilities of faith in your work for Him as you realize the strength of your weakness and the might of your God, for it is "not by might, nor by power, but by my spirit, saith the Lord of Hosts."

The day has come for God to reveal Himself through the very weakness of His instruments, and to prove once more that He has chosen the foolish things of the world to confound the wise, and the weak things to confound the things that are mighty.

5. All difficulties and dangers must give way before the omnipotence of faith. By faith the walls of Jericho fell down after they had been compassed seven days, and still the mightiest citadels of the adversary must give way before the steadfast and victorious march of faith. By faith Daniel stopped the mouths of lions and was delivered, we are expressly told, because he believed in his God. It was not his uprightness of life, or courageous fidelity that saved him, but his confidence in Jehovah. Such faith has carried the intrepid Arnot through the jungles of Africa and delivered the heroic Paton from the murderous fury of the savages of Tanna, and held back the stroke of death and the threatened disaster from many of us in the humbler experiences of our providential lives. Still the God of faith is as near, as mighty, and as true as when He walked with the Hebrew children through the fire, and guarded the heroic Paul through all the perils of his changeful life. There is no difficulty too small for its exercise, and there is no crisis too terrible for its triumph. Shall we go forth with this shield and buckler, and prove all the possibilities of faith? Then indeed shall we carry a charmed life even through the very hosts of Hell, and know that we are immortal till our work is done.

6. All the victories of prayer are possible to him that believeth. "Whatsoever ye shall ask in prayer, believing, ye shall receive." "When ye pray believe that ye receive the things that ye ask and ye shall have them." It is not the strength or the length of the prayer that prevails but the simplicity of its confidence. It is the prayer of faith that claims the healing power of the unchanging Saviour.

It is the prayer of faith that reaches the soul that no human hand, perhaps, can approach, and sometimes brings from Heaven the answer before the echo of the petition has died away. Yonder in the city of Cleveland a broken-hearted wife is praying with an evangelist for her husband's soul. At that very hour an influence all unknown to himself is leading him into a prayer meeting in Chicago at noon, and before that prayer is ended the choirs of Heaven are singing over a repentant soul, and the Holy Ghost is whispering to her heart that the work is accomplished, not less surely than when on the morrow the swift mail brings the glad tidings from his own hand. The prayer of faith has reared those enduring monuments on Ashley Down where two thousand orphan children were fed every day by the hand of God alone, in answer to the humble, believing cry of a faithful minister. These are but patterns of what God has always been ready to do and hindered only by His people's unbelief. Beloved, these possibilities are open to each of us. We may not be called to public service, or qualified for instructive speech, or endowed with wealth and influence, but to each of us is given the power to touch the hand of omnipotence and minister at the golden altar of prevailing prayer. One censer only we must bring—the golden bowl of faith, and as we fill it with the burning coals of the Holy Spirit's fire, and the incense of the great High Priest, lo there will be silence once again in Heaven, as God hushes the universe to listen, and then the living fire will be poured out upon the earth in the mighty forces of providence and grace, by which the kingdom of our Lord is to be ushered in.

7. All peace and joy are possible to him that believeth. The apostle's prayer for the Romans is that the God of hope shall fill them with all joy and peace in believing. It is God's will and purpose that the unbelieving soul

shall be an unhappy soul, and that he shall be kept in perfect peace whose mind is stayed on God and trusting in Him. Would you then know the peace that passeth all understanding? Be careful for nothing and steadfastly believe that the Lord is at hand, supreme above every circumstance, and causing all things to work together for good to them that love Him. Would you be happy in the darkest hour? Then trust in the Lord and stay yourself upon your God. Would you have the perennial overflowings of joy? Then learn to say "Though now ye see him not, yet believing, ye rejoice with joy unspeakable and full of glory." The joy of mere paroxysmal emotion is like the cut flower of a brief winter's day, separated from the root and withering before another sun goes down. The joy of faith is the fruit and perpetual bloom that covers the living tree, or springs from the rooted plant in the watered garden.

"The men of faith have found
Glory begin below—
Celestial fruit on hostile ground
From faith and hope may grow."

8. The evangelization of the world is to be given to faith. The most successful missionary operations of today are sustained wholly through faith in God and the power of prayer. There is no field for faith so vast and so sublime as the mission field today, and there is no limit to the possibilities which faith may claim. Oh that some of us may rise to the magnitude of this great opportunity and become workers together with God for the greatest achievement of all the Christian centuries.

9. The Lord's coming will doubtless be given at last to faith. There will be a generation who shall say, "Lo! this is our God, we have waited for him." As yet it is our blessed hope but it will some day become more. And

reading both upon earth and sky the tokens of His coming, His waiting bride shall hear the glad cry, "The marriage of the Lamb is come." To Simeon of old it was made known that he should see the Lord's Christ, and to some shall be given in the last times the Morning Star that shall precede the Millennial dawn. The Lord help us so to understand our times and the work the Master expects of us to prepare His coming, that we shall be permitted to share its glorious recompense of faith and even hasten that joyful day.

10. But beyond all that has been said this promise means that *all* things are possible to him that believeth. It is possible to have any or even many of the achievements specified and yet miss the all things of God's highest will. The meaning of this promise in its fullness is that faith may claim a complete life, a blessing from which nothing shall be lacking, a finished service, and a crown from which no jewel of recompense shall be found wanting. There are lives which are not wholly lost, and yet are not saved to the uttermost. There are rainbows whose arch is broken, but there is a rainbow round about the throne whose perfect circle is the type of a completed record and an infinite reward. Many of us are coming short of all that God has had in His highest thought for us. When the king of Israel stood by the bedside of the dying prophet of the Lord, Elisha put his hand upon the hands of Joash and helped him shoot the arrows which were symbolic of faith and victory; but then the prophet required that the king should follow up this act of mutual faith by a more individual expression of the measure of his own expectation. Alas, like most of us, his faith evaporated long before its needed work was done. He smote thrice upon the ground and then he stayed. Too late for him to recover his lost blessing, the grieved and

angry prophet upbraided him for his negligence and narrowness of heart, and told him sorrowfully that his blessing should be limited according to the measure of his own little faith. Never shall I forget the solemnity with which God brought this passage to my soul in a crisis of my life, and asked how much I would take from him and how little would satisfy my faith. Thank God He enabled me to say with a bursting heart, "nothing less than all Thy highest thought and will, even the all things of faith's greatest possibilities." The Lord help us to look forward ever to the time when all these opportunities shall be passing from our grasp, and to live each day under the power of those holy aspirations whose true value we shall then be able to understand, and evermore to say with Him who cherished the same lofty ambition, "I count not my life dear unto myself that I may finish my course with joy." Beloved, are you missing anything out of your life, your one precious, narrow span of earthly opportunity, the pivot on which eternity revolves, the one eternal possibility that never will return again? God is waiting to give you all, and all things are possible to him that believeth.

II. The reasonableness of faith. Why should God make all things dependent upon our faith?

1. Because the ruin of the race began with the loss of faith and its recovery must come through the exercise of faith. The poison Satan injected into the blood of Eve was a question of God's faithfulness, and the one prescription that the Gospel gives to unsaved sinners is, "Believe on the Lord Jesus Christ and thou shalt be saved."

2. Faith is the law of Christianity, the vital principle of the Gospel dispensation. The law of faith the apostle calls it in distinction from the law of works. The Lord Jesus expressed it in the simple formula which has become

the standard of answered prayers and every blessing that we receive through the name of Jesus. God is therefore bound to act according to our faith and also according to our unbelief.

3. Faith is the only way known to us by which we can accept a gift from God, and inasmuch as all the blessings of the Gospel are the gifts of grace, they must come to us through faith and in the measure of our faith, if they come at all.

4. Faith is necessary as a subjective influence to prepare our own hearts for the reception of God and His grace. How can the Father communicate His love to a timid, trembling heart? How can God come near to a frightened child? I have seen a little bird die of terror in my hand, when I intended it no harm but tried in vain to caress it and win its love. And so the individual heart without faith would die in the presence of God in absolute terror, and be unable to receive the overflowing love of the Father which it could not understand.

5. Faith is an actual spiritual force. It is no doubt one of the attributes of God Himself. We find it exemplified in Jesus in all His miracles. He explains to His disciples that it was the very power by which He withered the fig tree and the power by which they could overcome and dissolve the mightiest obstacles in their way. There is no doubt that while the soul is exercising through the power of God the faith that commands what God commands, that a mighty force is operating at that very moment upon the obstacle, a force as real as the currents of electricity or the power of dynamite. God has really put into our hands one of His own implements of omnipotence and permitted us to use it in the name of Jesus according to His will and for the establishment of His Kingdom.

6. The preëminent reason why God requires faith, is because faith is the only way through which God Himself

can have absolute room to work, for faith is just that colorless and simple attitude by which man ceases from his own works and enters into the work of God. It is the difference between the human and the divine, the natural and the supernatural. The reason therefore why faith is so mighty and indeed omnipotent is that it just makes way for the omnipotence of God. Therefore the two sentences are strangely and exactly parallel. "All things are possible with God," "all things are possible to him that believeth." The very same power is possessed by God and him that believeth, and the reason is that the latter is lost in, and wholly identified with, the former. How shall we illustrate the mighty distance between the earthly and the heavenly, the human and the divine, the finite and the infinite? Someone has said, take the strongest piece of artillery, load it to the muzzle with powder or dynamite, put in it the most perfect steel ball, be sure you have all the latest improvements in advance, then fire it, and your bullet will sweep through space at the rate of six hundred feet in a second. But in that same second, let God with a single flash of light and without a sound, propel a ray from yonder sun or star or midnight lamp, and it will fly six hundred thousand miles. Six hundred feet, six hundred thousand miles! This is a feeble figure of the difference between the human and the divine. That ponderous gun with its slow but destructive power is a type of man's works. That gentle sunbeam and light-beam with its silent, swift, beneficent ministry is a type of God's infinite resources. This is the world into which faith introduces us. Surrendering its own insufficiency it links itself with the all-sufficiency of God, and goes forth triumphantly exclaiming, "I can do all things through Christ which strengtheneth me," while approving Heaven echoes back "All things are possible to him that believeth."

III. The possibility of faith. "If thou canst believe."

1. Of course we need scarcely say that faith is dependent upon obedience and rightness of heart and life. We cannot trust God in the face of willful sin, and even an unsanctified state is fatal to any high degree of faith, for the carnal heart is not the soil in which it can grow, but it is the fruit of the Spirit, and is hindered by the weeds of sin and willful indulgence. The reason that a great many Christians have so little faith is because they are living in the world and in themselves, and separated in so large a part of their life from God and holiness. When the Lick Observatory was built on the Pacific coast, it was necessary to go above the valleys and lowlands of the coast, where the fogs and mists hung heavily over the land, and select a site on the top of Mount Hamilton, above the fogs and vapors of the ground, and in clear, unobstructed view of the heavens. So faith requires for its heavenly vision, the highlands of holiness and separation, and the clear, pure sky of a consecrated life.

Beloved, may you find in this the explanation of many of your doubts and fears, that your plane is too low, your heart is too mixed, and your life is too near this "present evil world."

2. Faith is hindered by the weak and unscriptural way in which so many excuse their unbelief and lightly think and speak of the sin of doubting God. If we would have strong faith we must recognize it as an imperative and sacred obligation, and steadfastly and firmly believe God, and refuse ever to doubt Him. Let us not say we cannot believe. It is true, we cannot of ourselves, but God has provided for us the power to believe if we will choose to do so. Let us then no more condone and palliate our doubts as harmless infirmities and sad misfortunes, but "take heed lest there be in any of us an evil heart of unbelief in departing from the living God."

3. Faith is hindered by reliance upon human wisdom, whether our own or the wisdom of others. The devil's first bait to Eve was an offer of wisdom, and for this she sold her faith. "Ye shall be as gods," he said, "knowing good and evil," and from the hour she began to know she ceased to trust. It was the spies that lost the land of promise to Israel of old. It was their foolish proposition to search out the land, and find out by investigation whether God had told the truth or not, that led to the awful outbreak of unbelief that shut the doors of Canaan to a whole generation. It is very significant that the names of these spies are nearly all suggestive of human wisdom, greatness and fame. And so in the days of Christ, it was the bondage of the Jews to the traditions of the fathers and the opinions of men, that kept them back from receiving Him. "How can ye believe," He asked, "which receive honor from men, and seek not that which cometh from God only?" This, today, has much to do with the limitations of the church's faith. The Bible is measured by human criticism, and the promises of God are weighed in the balance of natural probability and human reason. Our own wisdom is just as dangerous if it takes the place of God's simple word, and therefore, if we would trust the Lord with all our heart, we must lean not to our own understanding.

4. Self-sufficiency and dependence on our strength is also a hindrance to our faith.

God, therefore, has to reduce us to helplessness before we can have much trust in Him. The hour of His mightiest interposition is usually the time of our greatest extremity.

A secular weekly tells the story of a little fellow whose experience represents that of a good many older people. He had reached that epoch in a boy's life when he gets his first pants, and the uplift unsettled his spiritual equilibrium. Hitherto he had been a devout little Christian and usually joined his little sister every morning in asking the Lord's help and blessing for the day, but this morning when he looked at his new pants, and felt himself a man, he stopped his little sister as she began to pray for him as usual, "Lord Jesus, take care of Freddie today, and keep him from harm," and like poor Simon Peter, in his own self-sufficiency he cried out, "No, Jennie, don't say that; Freddie can take care of himself now." The little saint was shocked and frightened, but knew not what to do. And so the day began, but before noon they both climbed up into a cherry tree and while reaching out for the tempting fruit, Freddie went head foremost down into an angle between the tree and the fence, and with all his desperate struggles and his frightened sister's, he was utterly unable to extricate himself, and at last he looked up to Jennie with a look of mingled shame and intelligence and said, "Jennie, pray; Freddie can't take care of himself after all." Just then a strong man was coming along the road and the answer to their prayer quickly came as the sturdy arms in a few minutes had taken down the fence and Freddie was free, and went forth with a lesson for life, to walk like Simon Peter, with downward head and humble trust in a strength and care more mighty than his own.

Truly this is the soil of faith! Wisely said Habakkuk, centuries ago, as he contrasted pride and confidence, "His soul which is lifted up is not upright in him: but the just shall live by his faith."

Beloved, has God brought you to the end of your strength? Rejoice and be exceeding glad, for it is the beginning of His Omnipotence, if faith will but fall into His mighty arms and cry like those of old, "Lord, it is nothing with Thee to help by many or with those who have no power. Help us Lord, for in Thy Name we go against this great multitude."

5. Faith is hindered by sight and sense, and our foolish dependence upon external evidences.

The very evidence in which we must live and grow is the unseen, and therefore all outward things must be withdrawn before we can truly believe; and as we look not at the things which are seen but on the things which are not seen, they grow real, more real than the things of sense and then God makes them real in actual accomplishment. But faith must first step out into the great unknown, and walk upon the water to go to Jesus, nay, walk upon the air; but where was something only void it will find the rock beneath, like the traveler in the Alps who had reached the end of the mountain path as it suddenly disappeared beneath a great mass of ice and snow and became a subterranean torrent, while the mountain rose sternly in front and the miles of desolation which he had traveled lay behind. What should he do? Suddenly his guide exclaimed, "Follow me!" and plunged into the descending torrent and then disappeared from his view under the great mountain which it tunnelled. It was an awful venture, but he must either follow or die, and plunging in, there was a sudden shock, and the whirl of waters and blackness of darkness, and then a burst of light, and he was lying on the banks of a quiet stream on the other side of the mountain, in the sweet valley below. The unseen way had led to life and light.

So faith still walks in paths of mystery ofttimes, but God will always make it plain. Is not this the hindrance to your faith that you hesitate to believe before you venture upon the naked word of promise? Your faith alone is the substance of things hoped for, the evidence of things not seen. God help us to walk by faith and not by sight!

Therefore God has to train us in the way of faith by difficulties, trials, and seeming refusals, until like the Syro-Phœnician woman, we simply trust on and refuse to be refused. He is always waiting to recompense our trust by the glad words, "Great is thy faith! Be it unto thee even as thou wilt."

6. Finally, this faith is hindered most of all by what we call "our faith," and our fruitless struggles to work out a faith which after all is but a make-believe and a desperate trying to trust God, which must ever come short of His vast and glorious promise. The truth is that the only faith that is equal to the stupendous promises of God and the measureless needs of our life, is "the faith of God" Himself, the very trust which He will breathe into the heart which intelligently expects Him as its power to believe, as well as its power to love, obey, or perform any other exercise of the new life.

Blessed be His name! He has not given us a chain which reaches within a single link of our poor helpless heart, but that one last link is fatal to all the chain. Nay, the last link, the one that fastens on the human side is as divine as the link that binds the chain of promise to His Throne of promise in the heavens. "Have the faith of God," is His great command. "I live by the faith of the Son of God" is the victorious testimony of one who had proved it true.

Beloved, in the light of this great provision, listen to the mighty promise now, and in His faith rise to claim, "If thou canst, believe. All things are possible to him that believeth," and cry, "Lord, I believe, nay, not I, but Thou! Help Thou my unbelief."

And now, beloved, this mighty engine of spiritual power is placed in our hands by Omnipotent love. Shall we claim, and by the help of God, rise to its utmost possibilities, and shall we from this hour turn it, like a heavenly weapon, upon the field of Christian life and conflict, and use it for all to which God has called us in the great conflicts of the age and for the Kingdom of our Lord and Saviour Jesus Christ? Our lot has fallen upon momentous times; the last decade of this stupendous century has just begun, and it finds the Church of God awaking to the greatest campaign of the Christian centuries, the evangelization of the world, with a view to the preparation for our Lord's immediate coming. What a glorious possibility! It is one of the possibilities of faith.

Last night as I sat at my open window, far into the night watches, from one of the cottages yonder, I heard the voice of prayer go forth all night long. It was a ceaseless and mighty cry that the mighty God would work with all His power and glory, and though the same words were oft repeated by the same voice, it never seemed to grow monotonous, for there was so much that language could not express in that prayer that it touched my heart with tenderness and solemnity, and seemed like a prophecy of that which I trust is to go forth from this mighty convocation and be caught up by all the world until it shall be answered by the voices of heaven above, proclaiming, "The kingdoms of this world have become the kingdom of our Lord and of His Christ. Alleluia! The Lord God Omnipotent reigneth." Oh, shall we take this engine of omnipotence, the prayer of faith, and turn it toward the heavens, and turn it upon the earth, and turn it against every foe, until we shall find it wholly true, "All things are possible to him that believeth."

It has been proposed that we should form, this day, a Prayer Alliance, for the evangelization of the world during this present century, and the speedy coming of our Lord Jesus. Beloved, can there be a grander opportunity for the practical application of this great theme, and shall we not with one heart, join hands in believing prayer, around the world, until the happy day when we shall join hands once more around the Millennial Throne and praise Him for the glorious fulfillment?

II

The Joy of the Lord

"The joy of the Lord is your strength" [Nehemiah 8:10].

THERE is no more pointed difference between Christianity and all other religions than the element of joyfulness.

The natural countenance of heathenism is gloomy, and often profoundly sad. The true expression of a consecrated face is radiance and gladness. True, this is not always realized as it ought to be, but when the Holy Spirit shines in the consecrated heart, the face will reflect its glory, and, like Stephen's, be often like the face of an angel. The reporter of a weekly paper once remarked as he described the services of one of our happy conventions, "one thing that characterized all the faces was their wondrous joyousness." Surely this ought to be ever true! Look at those two sisters, born of one mother, rocked in one cradle, educated in one school, yet parted now by a distance far greater than leagues can measure. The younger sister is rich, prosperous, admired by a wide circle of friends, loved by every member of her family, and indulged in every gratification that social position or ample wealth can procure. The other is poor; her life is a struggle with circumstances, her time is crowded with toil and care; her dearest friends often misunderstand her religious attitude, and rudely blame her for the very things which are the highest services and sacrifices of her love. And yet her face shines with a deep, transparent joy, compared with which the other is dull and tame. The daughter of wealth and prosperity has become so used to her surroundings that they are no more to her than the humble circumstances of the other are to her. External luxuries have palled her appetite long ago, and no deeper springs have opened in her empty heart. Look at her when circumstances change! She has no other resources. Bereavement and death find her without consolation, and when she loses earth she loses all she had, and the parting is the more terrible in proportion to the pleasure of the possession. But the other has an inner source of peace and happiness that external vicissitudes cannot affect. Her trials throw her more wholly upon that hidden source of joy, and when all else is over shadowed with darkness, you may often see her face, as it were the face of an angel, and when sobs and tears are heard on every side, around her dying couch, her voice is melodious with praise, and her face is shining with the reflected glory of the everlasting day.

Why should it not be so? "God is Light, and in him is no darkness at all." The blessed God must be the source of blessedness. His Beloved Son, our Pattern and our Saviour, is the Prince of Peace, and the Royal Bridegroom, whom God "hath anointed with the oil of gladness above his fellows," and surely His salvation should be a glad salvation; His touch should bring joy and sunshine, and they who follow Him should be true to His own ideal of that happy company who "shall come to Zion with songs and everlasting joy; they shall obtain joy and gladness, and sorrow and sighing shall flee away." As we look over the earth we find that God has put beauty and gladness wherever He can. He has made us to be happy, and He has sent redemption to restore and consummate our joy, and so His great salvation is inseparably linked with a rejoicing spirit. True, it can stoop to sorrow; it will enter the saddest home and the darkest midnight, but it cannot dwell with gloom. It must banish sorrow as well as sin, and live in the light of joy.

And so we must give up trying to combine religion and

melancholy, for Christ will have none but a happy people. Even old Judaism robed itself in bridal garments whenever it could and went forth with songs of rejoicing. Under the Mosaic law there was a constant succession of feasts, and the whole nation was required every little while to go on a great religious picnic to keep them from settling down into selfishness and melancholy. And in the closing festival of the sacred year they were required to spend an entire week in the most romantic and picturesque religious rejoicings, dwelling in rustic booths and uniting in festal services and sacred songs and ceremonies, which must have formed a grand and impressive spectacle of national rejoicing.

It was this Feast of Tabernacles that Nehemiah and the people were now observing, yet, like some of us, they had come with long faces, and thought it becoming to celebrate the occasion by a few appropriate tears, as they thought of the desolations of Zion which had just been removed and restored. But Nehemiah told them that it was no time for mourning, simply because it was a holy day, and holiness and tears did not go well together; that the sorrows were past, and therefore there was no cause for mourning any longer, but this was a day for gladness and praise, and the spirit of praise was necessary in order even to their own preparation and strength for the tasks in which they were engaged; "for, the joy of the Lord," he declares, "is your strength."

I. The Source of Strength

1. This is true of us also, even in connection with the ordinary duties of daily life. How much one can do when the heart is light and free, and how long and heavy the easiest task when it is irksome! That mother can toil half the night, that father can sweat all the day, for the

joy of knowing that it is for the child of his love. Listen to the words of the sailors as they heave their heavy loads into the hold of yonder vessel with their ringing chorus sometimes of two syllables; but if it is only Ho-Hay, they sing it and they sing it in unison, and the great packages seem like feathers in their hands. Look at the soldiers as they march over the long tramp of many miles! But the beat of the drum or the chorus of their battle songs lighten up all the toil of the way.

Quaint old John Bunyan puts it happily when he tells us how he wrote the *Pilgrim's Progress* in his old Bedford dungeon. "So I was had home to prison," he goes on to say, "and I sat me down and wrote and wrote, because joy did make me write." The old dungeon with its stinted rays of light, its clumsy table, its wooden stool, its pallet of straw, was heaven to him because the joy of the pilgrim and the pilgrim's home and the pilgrim's story were bursting in his happy heart. Oh, how we need this joy amid the plod and the drudgery of every week, in the factory, the shop, over the counter, in the kitchen, at the desk, on the street, on the farm, and we may add, in what is often the harder places of public life, and the weary monotony of publicity, and the great heartless noisy world! But, thank God! Circumstances will make little difference where the everlasting springs are bursting from the deep well of His joy in the heart.

> The joy of the Lord is our strength for life's burden,
> And gives to each duty a heavenly zest;
> It will set to sweet music the task of the toiler,
> And soften the couch of the laborer's rest.

David has beautifully expressed this blending of common life with heavenly gladness in one of the psalms, where he says, "Thy statutes have been my songs in the house of my pilgrimage." Statutes are just precepts of daily duty and David enjoyed them by setting them to music and translating them to ceaseless praise. This, in a word, is the meaning of the one hundred and nineteenth psalm. It is all about duty, and yet it is the most exquisitely constructed in the Hebrew Psalter. As it has been well said, it is duty set to music.

This is the way to make duty easy and acceptable to God. I have known a servant girl whose life was intolerable, and whose mistress was regarded as a petty tyrant, become so happy in the same home and with the same woman after she received the baptism of the Holy Spirit that she would not have exchanged her place for any other, and her mistress actually came to her to ask what had happened, and became an earnest inquirer through her beautiful transformation.

Beloved, let us take the joy of the Lord into the dark places and the hard places and the low places, and the dusty, grimy streets and lanes of life! Let us plant the flowers around the little cottage as well as the great mansion! Let us have the song of the birds along the wayside, and even in the night, as well as in the gilded cage of the drawing room and in the broad sunshine of the day! Let us rejoice in the light evermore and go through the pathways of common life so filled with the Spirit that like men intoxicated with the wine of heaven, we shall be heard "speaking to ourselves in psalms and hymns and spiritual songs, singing with grace in our hearts to the Lord," and then it shall be true, "Whatsoever ye do in word or deed," we shall "do all in the name of the Lord Jesus, giving thanks unto God and the Father by him."

2. The joy of the Lord is our strength for the trials of life. There are two ways of bearing a trial; the one is the spirit of stoical endurance and the other through the counteracting forces of a holy and victorious joy. It was thus that Christ endured the cross for the joy that was set

before Him, and then He could despise the shame and not even allow the smell of fire to remain upon His garments. We read in the first chapter of Colossians the prayer of the apostle for a company of saints who had already reached such a measure of holiness that they were made partakers of the inheritance of the saints in light; but there was something higher and better for them, namely, that they should be "strengthened according to his glorious power unto all patience and longsuffering with joyfulness." "Patience" to endure the trials that come from the hand of God, and "longsuffering" to endure those which come from men and both to be endured with real joyfulness. In fact, there is nothing to endure when the heart is full of joy. It lifts us wholly above the trial, and we do not realize that we are being afflicted or wronged. The blessedness of true self-sacrifice is in being so filled with God that we will not have any sacrifice. What luxury of grace it is thus to be lifted above all that could even try the heart! The rocks are not taken from the bottom of the stream, but the blessed tides rise so high that the ships sail far above them in the current of God's great joy. And so the apostle explains his self-sacrifices for the Philippians, "Though I be offered on the sacrifice and service of your faith, I joy and rejoice with you all."

The Hebrew Christians were congratulated that they had been enabled to take "joyfully the spoiling of their goods." This is not a very common experience. Some good women lose their sanctification over a set of smashed dishes by a careless servant, or the spilling of coffee over the new tablecloth or dress, or the spots on the little dresses of heedless children; and some men get very angry over the mistakes or failures of employees or servants that injure their business or lose large sums of money.

Sir Isaac Newton once lost all the calculations of twenty-five years by the burning of a lot of papers through the carelessness of a little dog, and the world remembers him with more admiration than for all his discoveries because he simply answered, "Poor thing! You little know the mischief you have done."

The joy of the Lord always counts on something better than we lose, and remembers that there is one above who is the great Recompenser and Restorer, and will give a thousand times more later for one victory of patience and love than all the world is worth today.

> Yes, the joy of the Lord is our strength for life's trials,
> And lifts the crushed heart above sorrow and care,
> Like the nightingale's song, it can sing in the darkness,
> And rejoice when the fig tree is withered and bare.

3. The joy of the Lord is our strength for temptation. "Count it all joy," James says, "when ye fall into divers temptations." One reason for this is because it is the best way to meet them. The devil always gets the best of a melancholy soul. Despondency will always bring surrender. Satan is so little used to joy in his own home that a happy face always scares him away. Amalek got hold of the hindmost of Israel's camp, the discouraged ones who were dragging behind and fretting about the hot weather and the hard road they had to travel. Such people always find the way harder before they get through. The fiery serpents, which were the devil's scouts, stung the murmuring multitudes, and it was an upward look to the brazen serpent that healed them. Jehoshaphat's armies marched to battle and victory with shouts of faith and songs of praise, and so still the joy of the Lord is the best equipment for the great conflict. But the apostle also means, no doubt, that temptation is no cause for despondency, but rather a great opportunity of spiritual

progress. It is the proving of our armor and an evident token that the devil sees something in us worth trying to steal, and we may be very sure where the army of the enemy is encamped there the army of the Lord is also near. "The trying of our faith worketh patience but let patience have her perfect work." Let us go through all the discipline and learn all that it has to teach us. "When he is tried, he shall receive the crown of life, which the Lord hath promised to them that love him."

Let us then go forth into the conflicts which await us without a fear of cloud, and when we cannot feel the joy, but "are in heaviness through manifold temptations," let us "count it all joy," and say, "I will rejoice in the Lord, and I will be joyful in my God."

> The joy of the Lord is our strength for temptation,
> And counts it the testing of patience and grace;
> It marches to battle with shouts of salvation,
> And rides o'er its foes in the chariots of praise.

4. The joy of the Lord is our strength for the body. "A merry heart doeth good like a medicine." This is the divine prescription for a weak body. And so on the other hand, despondency and depression of spirits are the cause of nervousness, headache, heartbreak, and low physical vitality. A word of cheer and an impulse of hope and gladness will often break the power of disease.

I remember a dying man whom I visited in the earliest years of my ministry, who was given up by his physicians and pronounced in a dying condition, so that they gave up the case and expected his death during the night. But as I visited him, as I supposed for the last time, and tenderly led him to the Saviour, and as he accepted the gospel and became filled with the peace of God and the joy of salvation, there came upon him such a baptism of glory and such an inspiration of the very rapture of heaven, that he kept us for hours beside his bed as he shouted and sung, what we all believed to be the beginning of the songs of heaven, and we bad him farewell long after midnight, fully expecting that our next meeting would be above. But so mighty was the uplift in that soul that his body, unconsciously to himself, threw off the power of disease, and the next morning he was convalescent, to the amazement of his physicians, and in a few days entirely well. I knew nothing, at that time, of divine healing, but simply witnessed with astonishment and delight, the power of divine joy to heal disease. Many a time since have I seen the healing and the gladness of Jesus come together to the soul and body, and the night of weeping turned into a morning of joy. Many a time have I seen the darkly clouded and diseased brain lighted up with the joy of the Lord, and saved from insanity by a baptism of holy gladness.

It is true there is a deeper cause and a more divine power than the mere natural influence of joy. Incurable disease can only yield to the actual touch of divine omnipotence, but joy is the channel through which the healing waters flow, and the overflow of the life of Christ in both soul and body. If you would live above your physical conditions, if you would renew your strength continually and "mount up on wings as eagles, and run and not be weary, and walk and not faint," if you would carry in your veins the exhilaration and zest of unwearied youth and freshness, if you would know, even here, in all its fulness, the foretaste of the resurrection life in your body, if you would be armed against the devil's shafts of infirmity and pain, and throw off his arrows upon your body as the heated iron repels the water which will not lie upon it, then, beloved, "Rejoice, in the Lord alway: and again I say, Rejoice."

To return to our figure—the humblest housewife knows

that water cannot rest upon a red-hot stove cover, but leaps and dances over it in consternation, and flies off in explosions of helpless effervescence. So the devil will try in vain to pour cold water upon your life and work, and even your frame, if you keep ever in the white heat of heavenly joy.

5. The joy of the Lord is our strength for service and testimony. It makes all our work easy and delightful. It gives a perpetual spring in the hardest fields of Christian service. It goes with the city missionary and the all-night worker in the dives and slums, and takes away the natural shrinking from the degraded and unclean, the horror of filth and vermin, the fear of violent and wicked men and all the repulsiveness and hideousness of the surrounding scenes; and it makes the work, that naturally would be revolting, a perfect fascination, and enables the consecrated heart to say, "None of these things move me, neither count I my life dear unto myself, so that I might finish my course with joy, and the ministry, which I have received of the Lord Jesus, to testify of the gospel of the grace of God."

Not only does it give a constraining motive to our service, but it also gives it a divine effectiveness and power. It illuminates the face with the light of heaven, and melts the voice with accents of tenderness and love. It gives our words a weight and winning power which men cannot gainsay. They know that we possess a secret to which they are strangers, and our gladness awakens their longing to share our joy. A shining face and radiant spirit are worth a ton of logic, rhetoric and elocution. A poor crippled saint, standing up in a meeting and telling what God hath done for her soul, with a face divinely beautiful in all its homeliness, will bring more souls to Christ than the eloquence of a dozen college graduates without the joy of the Lord.

A scholarly minister once gave a course of lectures on the "Evidences of Christianity," for the special purpose of convincing and converting a wealthy and influential sceptic in his congregation. The gentleman attended his lectures and was converted, and a few days after the minister ventured to ask him which of the lectures it was that impressed him decisively. "The lectures!" answered the gentleman, "my dear sir, I don't even remember the subjects of your lectures, and I cannot say that they had any decisive influence upon my mind. I was converted by the testimony of a dear old colored woman who attended those services, and who, as she hobbled up the steps close to me, with her glad face, as bright as heaven, used to say, 'My blessed Jesus! my blessed Jesus!' and turning to me would ask, 'Do you love my blessed Jesus?' and that, sir, was my evidence of Christianity."

Bless the Lord! we can all shine like that, *burning,* as well as *shining* lights, and setting hearts aglow with the contagion of our joy. The world is looking for happiness and if it find the secret in a genuine form, will try to get it. Charles Finney tells us how the good deacons used to ask him in prayer meeting, when he attended it in his ungodly days, if he did not want them to pray for him. "No," he said, "I should be very sorry to have you pray for me. For, in the first place, if I were converted through your prayers I should be as miserable as you are; and in the next place, I do not believe that your prayers would have any power to bring about my conversion, and I suspect that you yourselves would be a good deal surprised if they had, for you have been praying in the same melancholy way ever since I came to this town, for a revival, and I can see by your tones and your faces that you have no idea that it is ever coming. When I am converted, I want a religion that will make me happy, and a God who will do what I ask him."

Beloved, the Lord save us from religious melancholia, and send us out to work for Him with shining faces, victorious accents, and hearts overflowing with contagious joy. Then, like Stephen, we will be able to look into the faces of our enemies and confound them by our very countenances, and force the world to take knowledge of us that we have been with Jesus.

> Let the joy of the Lord be the strength of our service,
> As it speaks in our faces and accents of love,
> As it wins the sad world to the fulness of Jesus,
> And draws hungry hearts His salvation to prove.

II. THE SECRET OF THIS JOY

1. It springs from the assurance of salvation. It is the joy of salvation. Its happy song is,

> "Blessed assurance, Jesus is mine,
> Oh, what a rapture of glory Divine!
> Heir of salvation, purchased of God,
> Born of His Spirit, washed in His blood.
> This is my story, this is my song,
> Praising my Saviour all the day long."

If you would know it you must accept His promise with full assurance of faith, and rest upon His word without a wavering or a doubt.

2. It is the joy of the Holy Ghost. "The fruit of the Spirit is love, joy." It is not indigenous to earthly soil; it is a plant of heavenly birth. It belongs to the kingdom of God, which is "righteousness, and peace and joy in the Holy Ghost." To know it we must receive the baptism of the Pentecostal Spirit in full surrender and simple faith. It is the characteristic of all who receive this baptism that they know the joy of the Lord, and until we do receive this eternal fountain in our heart, all our attempts at joy are but surface wells; they are waters often defiled and their bottom often dry. This is the great Artesian stream,

the "well of water" Jesus gives "springing up unto everlasting life."

3. It is the joy of faith. "Now the God of hope fill you with all joy and peace in believing." There is indeed a deep delight when God has answered prayer, and the joy of fulfillment and possession overflows with thankfulness, but there is a more thrilling joy when the heart first commits itself to His naked promise, and standing on His simple word in the face of natural improbability, or even seeming impossibility, declares, "though the figtree shall not blossom nor fruit be in the vines, yet will I rejoice in the Lord and joy in the God of my salvation." If you are doubting God you need not wonder that your joy is intermittent. The witness of the Spirit always follows the act of trust. "Thou wilt keep him in perfect peace, whose mind is stayed on thee: because he trusteth in thee," but it is just as true, "Surely, if ye will not believe, ye shall not be established."

4. The joy of the Lord is sustained by His word and nourished by His "exceeding great and precious promises." "I rejoice at thy word," exclaims the Psalmist, "as one that findeth great spoil." Oh, the rich delight of beholding in the light of the Holy Spirit, the heavenly landscape of truth open before the spiritual vision, like some land of promise shining in the glory of the sunlight, the whole Bible seeming like the vision Moses saw from Pisgah's top! We have found great spoil and it is all our own. "We have received the Spirit that we may know the things that are freely given us of God," and we can truly say like the Psalmist again, "Thy testimonies are the joy and rejoicing of my heart." How sweet the voice in which the Spirit speaks the promises to the sorrowing heart and makes this precious word a living voice from our Beloved!

Dear friends, do you know the joy that lies hidden in these neglected pages, the honey that you might drink from this garden of the Lord, these blossoms of truth and promise? Oh, take your Bibles as the living love-letters of His heart to you and ask Him to speak it to you in joy and faith and spiritual illumination, as the sweet manna of your spirit's life and the honey out of the Rock of Ages!

5. It is the joy of prayer. Its element is the closet, and its source the Mercy-seat. No prayerless life can be a happy one. "They that wait upon the Lord shall renew their strength; they shall mount up with wings as eagles." "Ask, and ye shall receive, that your joy may be full."

> "This is the place where Jesus sheds
> The oil of gladness on our heads;
> The place than all besides more sweet,
> It is the blood-bought Mercy-seat."

6. It is the joy of meekness and love. "For the meek shall increase their joy in the Lord," and the loving spirit ever finds that "it is more blessed to give than to receive." Selfishness is misery, love is life and joy. The gentle, lowly, chastened spirit shall find all the flowers in bloom and the waters flowing in the valleys of humility. The unselfish heart shall never fail to prove the promise true, "If thou draw out thy soul to the hungry, and satisfy the afflicted soul; . . : the Lord shall guide thee continually, and shall satisfy thy soul in drought, . . . and thou shalt be like a watered garden, and like a spring of water, whose waters fail not."

Beloved, do you know the gladness which comes from yielding to the will of God, or bearing patiently the wrong, from being silent under the word of reproach, from returning good for evil, from the word that comforts the sorrowing heart, from the cup of cold water to another given, from the sacrifice of your own indulgence that the saving may be given to Him? Oh, then it is that all the bells of joy are heard softly ringing and the Master whispers to the hearts that tremble with its gladness, "ye did it unto me."

7. It is the joy of service and especially of winning souls. All true work is a natural delight, but work for God in the true spirit and in the power of the Holy Ghost, is the very partnership of His joy, whose meat and drink it was to do the will of Him that sent Him and to finish His work. If you would have a life lifted above a thousand temptations and petty cares be busy for your Master, and let each moment see

> "Some work of love begun
> Some deed of kindness done,
> Some wanderer sought and won,
> Something for Thee."

We cannot convey the Living Water to another heart without being watered ourselves on the way. There is no joy more exqusite than the joy of leading a soul to Christ. It is like the mother's strange, instinctive rapture over her new-born baby. The other day a precious friend passed through the gates a few moments after her baby was born, but in the hour of her agony her very first word was, "How is my baby?" It was the first thrill of that strange delight which is the very touch of the love which the Holy Ghost will give us for the souls He permits us to win for Christ. It is indeed a spiritual motherhood, and it has all the joy and all the pain of a mother's love.

Beloved, do you know the ecstasy of feeling the new life of an immortal spirit sweeping through your very veins, as, kneeling by the side of one just born to die no more, you place it, as a new-born babe in the bosom of your Saviour? You may know this joy, and every Christian ought to know it a hundredfold. It is the joy of angels, setting all the harps of heaven ringing, and surely it were strange if it were not the higher joy of ransomed saints.

8. It is the joy of the faithful servant. There is a sense even here, in which as often as we are true to God and faithful to the call of duty and opportunity, His Spirit gives us a present reward and a baptism of joy, and whispers to the faithful heart, "Well done, good and faithful servant! Enter thou into the joy of thy Lord."

9. It is the joy of hope. "We rejoice in hope of the glory of God." It is the reflected light of the coming Sunrise and the Millennial Day. Except the death and resurrection of Jesus and the baptism of the Holy Ghost, there is nothing that sheds within the heart a diviner gladness, and on the brow a holier light, than the blessed hope of the Lord's Coming. It is indeed "a light in the dark place," the very Morning Star that presages the Rising Sun. Then let us in this blessed hope "life up our heads for our redemption draweth nigh."

10. And finally, it is the joy of Christ Himself within us. "These things have I spoken unto you, that my joy might remain in you, and that your joy might be full." This is the deepest secret of spiritual joy; it is the indwelling Christ Himself rejoicing in the heart as He rejoiced on earth even in the darkest hour of His life, and as now, in heaven, He realizes the fulfillment of His own Messianic words in the sixteenth psalm; "Therefore my heart is glad, and my glory rejoiceth: my flesh also shall rest in hope. For thou wilt not leave my soul in hell; neither wilt thou suffer thine Holy One to see corruption. Thou wilt show me the path of life: in thy presence is fulness of joy; at thy right hand there are pleasures for evermore." In the fulness of joy is reigning now and its tides are swelling and rising to the same level in every heart in which He dwells.

Walking along the ocean beach hundreds of feet from the shore you may dig a little hole in the dry sand, and it will fill with water. Underneath the sand the waters flow and fill the pool to the level of their source. And so the life that is hid with Christ in God is in constant contact with the fountain of life, and though the world may not always see the overflow, yet the heart's depths are ever filling and we only need to make room, and lo! The empty void, whether great or small, is full to the measure of the fulness of God. This, beloved, is why we beseech you to receive the indwelling Christ. He is the source of the River of the Water of Life that flows from the Throne of God and the Lamb, and those whose hearts are His temple can sing, no matter how the tempests rage and the fig-tree withers,

> "God is the Treasurer of my soul,
> The source of lasting joy;
> A joy which time cannot impair,
> Nor death itself destroy."

III Filled with the Spirit

"Be filled with the Spirit" [Eph. 5:18].
"Ye are complete [filled] in Him" [Col. 2:10].

THE emphatic word in both these verses is "filled." It is the Greek *plaroo* which means to fill full, so full that there will be no room left empty. This is the thought which, with the assistance of the Holy Spirit, we desire to impress in this message. It does not mean to have a measure of the Holy Spirit, and to know a good deal of Christ, but to be wholly filled with, and possessed by, the Holy Ghost, and utterly lost in the life and fulness of Jesus. It is the completeness of the filling which constitutes the very essence of the perfect blessing. A fountain half full will never become a spring. A river half full will never become a water power. A heart half filled will never know "the peace which passeth all understanding" and the power which flows from the inmost being, as "rivers of living water."

I. The Nature of This Filling

1. It is all connected with a living Person. We are not filled with an influence; we are not filled with a sensation; we are not filled with a set of ideas and truths; we are not filled with a blessing, but we are filled with a Person. This is very strange and striking. It is wholly different from all other teaching. Human systems of philosophy and religion all deal mainly with intellectual truths, moral conditions or external acts. Greek philosophy was a system of ideas; Confucianism is a system of morals; Judaism is a system of laws and ceremonies; Christianity all centres in a living Person, and its very essence is the indwelling life of Christ Him-

self. He was not only its Head and Founder, but He is forever its living Heart and Substance, and the Holy Spirit is simply the agent and channel through whom He enters, possesses and operates in the consecrated heart. This reduces Christian life to great simplicity. We do not need to be filled in a great many compartments, and with a great many different experiences, ideas, or influences, but, in the centre of our being to receive Him in His personal life and fullness, and then He flows into every part and lives out His own life in all the diversified experiences and activities of our manifold life.

In the one garden we plant the living seed and water it from the same great fountain, and lo! it springs up spontaneously with all the varied beauty and fruitfulness of the lily and the rose, the foliage plant and the fruit tree, the clinging jessamine and the spreading vine. We have simply to turn on the fertilizing spring and nature's spontaneous life bursts forth in all its beautiful variety.

This, by a simple figure, is Christ's theory of a deeper life. Our being is the soil, He is the seed, His Holy Spirit is the Fountain of living Waters, and "the fruit of the Spirit is love, joy, peace, long-suffering, gentleness, goodness, faith, meekness, temperance."

Out in the great West lie millions of acres of barren land. They are a great possibility, but practically fruitless and waste. Beneath the soil of these Saharas lie undeveloped riches, all that is needed being one single element that would develop them into fruitfulness. That element is water. Let the mountain stream be turned into yonder valley, let the irrigating channels spread their network over all their vast fields, and lo! you behold a paradise, as lovely as the streets of Salt Lake City or some of the sweet villages and towns of California, with a luxuriance of beauty such as none of our Eastern lands can show. The soil was empty and barren until it became filled with the seed and the springs, and then the transformation spring up with spontaneous luxuriance. So the human heart is not self-constituted or self-sufficient; it is a bare and barren possibility. It may struggle its best to develop itself, but it will only develop, as those western deserts the sage brush and stunted palm which cover them today. But give it two things. Drop into that soil the living Christ, and flood it with the water of the Spirit's fullness. Lo! It reaches the relization of its true idea, and the promise of His own simple parable is perfectly fulfilled, "He that abideth in me, and I in him, the same bringeth forth much fruit: for without me ye can do nothing."

Shall we then realize, beloved, that God has made each of us, not a self-contained world of power and perfection, but simply a capacity to receive Him, a shell to hold His fullness, a soil to receive His Living Seed and fertilizing streams, and to produce, in union with Him, the fruits of grace? And shall we realize, on the other hand, that God has so constituted Christ and the Holy Spirit, who is just the Spirit of Christ, as perfectly to meet and satisfy the capacities and possibilities of our being; so that, while we are nothing without Him, His life and grace equally require us for their full development. Into His living Son God has poured all His fullness, so that "in him dwelleth all the fulness of the Godhead bodily." The Holy Spirit has now become the great Reservoir and system of distributing pipes and channels through which His fullness flows into us, and there is nothing which God requires of a man, or which man can ever need in the varied exigencies of life but Christ possesses for us, and we may have an exact adjustment to our every need, by simply receiving Him. This is the meaning of that beautiful expression, "Of His fulness have all we received, even grace for grace. For the law was given by Moses, but grace and reality came by Jesus Christ." All other systems gave us merely the ideas of things or the commandments or laws which require them of us. But Christ brings the power to realize them and is Himself the reality and substance in our hearts and lives. He is the Great Typical Man. But He is more than a pattern or a type, exhibiting what we ought to be, and demanding our imitation. He is also the Living Head and Progenitor of the very life which He Himself exhibits, begetting it in each of us by a living impartation of His very being, and reproducing Himself in us by the very power of His own life, and then feeding and nourishing this life by the Holy Spirit out of His own being.

Christ's Person, therefore, is far more than a pattern. It is a power, a seed, a spring of Living Water, nay, the very substance and support of the life He requires of us.

2. This Person is the true fullness of every part of our life. The idea of filling implies universality and completeness in the range within which He fills us. We are not filled unless we are filled in every part. This is just what Christ proposes to do in our full salvation.

He fills all the requirements of our salvation, all the conditions involved in connection with our redemption, reconciliation, justification. He just takes the indictment against us and fills it in with His own precious atonement, and in His own blood writes, "Settled forever." He takes the broken law and the sad and humiliating record of our failures, omissions and transgressions, and fills it up with His own perfect righteousness and writes over all our record, "Christ is the end of the law for righteousness to every one that believeth," "Accepted in the Beloved;" "He was made sin for us who knew no sin that we might be made the righteousness of God in him."

And so "we are complete in him." "By one offering

he hath perfected forever them that are sanctified," and we are as fully saved as if we had never sinned.

Now beloved, the great thing is to realize right here that this is complete, and, at the very threshold, to begin to enter into the fullness of Christ by recognizing ourselves as fully justified and forever saved from all past sin and transgression through the complete redemption of Jesus Christ. The lack of fullness in our subsequent experience is largely due to doubts and limitations which we allow to enter here. Christ's work for our redemption was finished and when we accept it, it is a complete and eternal salvation.

Again, Christ fills the deeper need of sanctification. He has provided for this in His atonement and in the resources of His grace. It is all wrapped up in Him and must be received as a free and perfect gift through Him alone. "For of him are ye in Christ Jesus, who of God is made unto us sanctification." Is sanctification the death of the sinful self? Well, this has been crucified with Him already upon the Cross, and we have but to hand it over to Him in unreserved committal and He will slay it and bury it forever in His grave. Is sanctification a new life of purity, righteousness, peace and joy in the Holy Ghost? Still more emphatically is it true that Christ Himself must be our life, our peace, our purity, and our full and overflowing joy.

Again, He is the fullness of our heart life. There is no place so sacred to us as our affections, no place so claimed by the great adversary of our souls, and so impossible to regulate by our own power and will. But Christ will give us His heart as well as His Spirit, and will love in us with the love which loves "the Lord our God with all our heart and soul and strength and mind," and which loves "one another even as he has loved us." Oh, how blessed that we have One who will really fill all the delicate and infinitely difficult and varied requirements of these sensibilities and affections, which carry with them such a world of possibility for our own or others' weal or woe.

Again, Christ will fill all the needs of our intellectual life. Our mental capacities will never know their full wealth of power and spiritual effectiveness until they become simply the vessels of His quickening life, and these brains of ours are laid at His feet simply as the censers which are to hold His holy fire. He will think in us, remember in us, judge in us, impart definiteness and clearness to our conceptions of truth, give us the tongue of fire, the illustration that both illuminates and melts, the accent and tone of persuasiveness and sympathy, the power of quick expression and utterance, and all the equipment necessary to make us "workmen that need not to be ashamed, rightly dividing the word of truth." Not of course without diligent and faithful attention to His wise and holy teaching, as He leads us in His work to see at once our own shortcomings and His full purpose for us. We must be taught of God, and teaching is sometimes very gradual, and even slow; but "He will guide us into all truth," and "perfect that which concerneth" our education and preparation for His work and will; and the mind that the Holy Spirit quickens and uses shall accomplish results for God which all the brilliancy of human genius and the scholarship of human learning can never approach.

Again, He will fill the needs of our body, for His body has been constituted, by the resurrection from the dead, a perpetual source of physical energy, sufficient for every member of His body the church, and adapted to every physical function and every test that comes in the pressure of human life, and the experience of a world where every step is beset with the elements of disease, suffering and physical danger. Christ is the true life of a redeemed body, and His Holy Spirit is able so to quicken these mortal bodies, as He dwells within us, that they shall receive a supernatural vigor directly derived from our exalted Head.

Again, Christ will fill all the situations of providence and all the needs that arise in our secular callings and the circumstances of our daily life. There is not one of them that may not be recognized as coming from Him, and meant to prove His all-sufficiency in some new direction. Oh, had we the faith to see God in everything as it meets us day by day, every chapter of life's history would be a new story of the romance of heavenly love in its magical power to transform darkness into light, difficulty into triumph, sorrow into joy, and the earthly into the heavenly; and Christ would be enabled to manifest Himself in His grace and power to innumerable witnesses, who never hear of Him from a pulpit, or read the story of His grace in anything else but human lives, in whom they could thus behold Him.

Again Christ will fill our capacities for happiness. He is the fullness of our peace and joy. He is the true portion of the souls that He has made; and, wholly filled with Him, there is no room for either care or fear.

Finally, Christ will fill that fundamental need on which every other experience of His fullness depends, namely, the faith that receives Him. This too, is but the life of Christ within us, and our highest part in the life of faith is to so abandon even our highest and hardest efforts to trust God and so boldly venture that we can receive the very faith of God and claim the "all things that are possible to him that believeth."

3. To be filled with Christ is not only to be filled with the divine life in every part, but it is to be filled every moment. It is to take Him into the successive instants of our conscious existence and to abide in His fullness.

For this is not a reservoir but a spring. It is a life which is continual, active and ever passing on with an outflow as necessary as its inflow, and if we do not perpetually draw the fresh supply from the living fountain, we shall either grow stagnant or empty. It is, therefore, not so much a perpetual fulness as a perpetual filling.

It is true there are periodical experiences of spiritual elevation which are part of God's plan for our life in Christ, and are designed no doubt to lift us to a higher plane of abiding union with Him. There are the Pentecosts and second Pentecosts, the great freshets and flood-tides, all of which have their necessary place in the spiritual economy. But there is the continual receiving, breath by breath and moment by moment, between these long intervals and more marked experiences, which is even more needful to spiritual steadfastness and healthfulness. God would have us alive to all His approaches, and open to all the "precious things of heaven, the dew, and the deep that coucheth beneath, the precious fruits brought forth by the sun, the precious things put forth by the moon, the precious things of the earth and the fulness thereof." Such lives will find that there is no moment of existence, and no part of our being which may not be some minister of God and draw some blessing from Him.

II. THE EFFECTS OF THE DIVINE FILLING

1. It is the secret of holiness. There is a measure of the Holy Spirit's life in every regenerate soul, but it is when every part of our being is filled with His love and possessed for His glory that we are wholly sanctified, and it is this divine fullness which excludes and keeps out the power of sin and self, even as it was the descending cloud upon the tabernacle which left no room for Moses within.

Would you have continual purity of heart and thought

and feeling, and entire conformity to the will of God? "Be filled with the Spirit;" "and of his fulness have all we received, and grace for grace." Let the heavenly water flow into every channel of irrigation and by every garden bed and plant, until all the graces of our Christian life shall be replenished by His grace, and bloom like the garden of the Lord. Only abide in Him and have His abiding, and you shall bring forth all the fruit of the Spirit.

2. It is the secret of happiness. A heart half full is only full enough to make it conscious of its lack. It is when the cattle are filled that they lie down in the green pastures. "These things have I spoken unto you that my joy might remain in you and that your joy might be full."

3. It is the secret of power. The electric current can so fill a little wire that it will become a force to turn the great wheels of the factory, and the overflowing sluice of the village stream has power enough to run a score of factories all along the river banks, but it is simply because it is overflowing. Only full hearts accomplish effectual work for God. Only the overflow of our blessing blesses others.

III. THE CONDITIONS OF BEING FILLED

1. He has promised to fill the hungry. "Blessed are they which do hunger and thirst after righteousness: for they shall be filled." Many who read these lines are no doubt longing for this experience and thinking with discouragement of how far short they come. Dear friend, this deep desire is the very beginning of the blessing you seek, and already the Holy Spirit is at work preparing your heart for the answer to your cry. No soul finds the fullness of Jesus so speedily as the one that is most deeply conscious of its failure and its needs. Thank God for

that intense desire that will not let you rest short of His blessing.

An eastern caravan was overtaken once in the desert with the failure of the supply of water. The accustomed fountains were all dried, the oasis was a desert, and they halted an hour before sunset to find, after a day of scorching heat, that they were perishing for want of water. Vainly they explored the usual wells, for they were all dry. Dismay was upon all faces and despair in all hearts, when one of the ancient men approached the sheik and counselled him to unloose two beautiful harts that he was conveying home as a present to his bride, and let them scour the desert in search of water. Their tongues were protruding with thirst, and their bosoms heaving with distress. But as they were led out to the borders of the camp and then set free on the boundless plain, they lifted up their heads on high, and sniffed the air with distended nostrils, and then, with unerring instinct, with course as straight as an arrow, and speed as swift as the wind, they darted off across the desert. Swift horsemen followed close behind, and an hour or two later hastened back with the glad tidings that water had been found, and the camp moved with shouts of rejoicing to the happily discovered fountains.

So still there is a hart that can ever find the springs of living water. It is the heart that hungers and thirsts for God. Thank God, beloved, if you have this deep spiritual instinct in your soul! Follow it as it leads you to the Throne of grace, to wait, and cry, and receive, until you can say, "Satisfied with favor and full with the blessing of the Lord."

2. The empty are always filled. "He hath filled the hungry with good things, but the rich he hath sent empty away." "Blessed are the poor in spirit for theirs is the kingdom of heaven." "Having nothing and yet possess-

ing all things." This is the paradox of grace. We never can be filled until we have room for God. Every great blessing begins with a great sacrifice, a great severance, a great dispossessing. "He brought them out that he might bring them in." Abraham must let Lot have his choice before he can have his full inheritance. Isaac must be offered on Mount Moriah before God can make it the seat of His future temple. Moses must let go the honors and prospects of his Egyptian princedom before he can receive his great commission, the lasting honor of his life work. The heart must be emptied of self and the world before it can be filled with Jesus and the Holy Ghost. Probably each of us is as full as we can hold because the places God does not fill are crammed with something else and God finds no room. Are we willing to be emptied? "Make the valley full of ditches," is still the prophet's command, "and the valley shall be filled with water." Are we in the valley of humiliation, and have we opened in the valley the still deeper ditches of need and conscious insufficiency? In proportion as we can say, "I am not sufficient," we shall be able to add, "my sufficiency is of God." Have we not only emptied out the old pirate self-will and his crew of worldliness and sin, but also all the cargo of our own strength, faith and religious experience, and made room for Christ to be our All and in all always? Do we habitually cease from ourselves in everything and thus make it necessary for God to assume the responsibility and supply the sufficiency, and in this spirit of self-renunciation and absolute dependence are we growing poorer and richer every day?

3. The open heart shall be filled. "Open thy mouth wide and I will fill it." We know what it is for the flower-cup to close its petals and also to open to the sunlight, the dew and the refreshing shower. The heart has it susceptibilties and receptive sensibilities, but often it is so

tightened up with unbelief, doubt, fear, and self-consciousness that it cannot take in the love which God is waiting to pour out. Do we not know what it is to meet people, with a heart full of love, and find them all tightened up and heart-bound? We become conscious at once of the repulsion and feel all the fountains of our love obstructed and rolled back again upon our own aching hearts. They cannot receive us. It is like the mother who found her long-lost child after years of separation, but the child could not recognize the mother, and as she tried to awaken its response and to pour out the full tides of her bursting heart and found no recognition, but only the dull stare of strangeness and suspicion, and all her caresses and tender over-flowings of affection rejected and met with cold indifference and even recoil, her heart broke in grief and disappointment, and she wept and sobbed in agony.

The heart of God is pouring out His love to many a soul who cannot, will not, take it in. It does not know its Father. His face is strange. There seems no avenue to the dull earthly heart and even the love of God has cause to exclaim, "How often would I have gathered you as a hen gathereth her brood under her wings and ye would not!" I have seen a man dying for months simply because he could not swallow more than a single grain of food or spray of moisture. Many a Christian's spiritual larynx is just as shrunken, and millions are starving to death in the midst of plenty, because their hearts are not open to receive God. There must be confidence, trust, the love that draws near and takes, the faith that accepts and receives, and the quietness of spirit that stays long enough open to be wholly filled.

4. Again, we are filled by waiting upon the Lord in prayer, and especially in continued and persevering prayer. It was after they had waited upon the Lord that they were all filled with the Holy Ghost. Prayer is not only

an asking but also a receiving. Many of us do not wait long enough before the Lord to get filled. You can take your breakfast in half an hour, but you cannot be filled with the Holy Spirit as quickly. There should be seasons of special waiting upon the Lord for this very purpose, and then there should be a ceaseless abiding in the Lord for the quiet replenishing, moment by moment. The one may be compared to the great rain storms that flood the river, and the other to the ceaseless moisture of the air and the morning and evening dews. No child of God who, in a proper spirit, and with an entire self-surrender and trust, waits upon God for the full baptism of His Holy Ghost, will ever be disappointed, but we shall surely go forth from such seasons refreshed and over-flowing with the love and life of God, and will find that special influences of power and blessing will follow such seasons, both in our own lives and the lives of others.

5. Service for God and for others is perhaps the most effectual condition of receiving continually the fullness of the Spirit. As we pour out the blessing God will pour it in. We have a pump in one of our institutions which is worked by steam. We have a way of always knowing when the reservoir on the roof is full. There is a little tell-tale downstairs which begins to run and a little bell to ring. Then we know that the over-flow has begun, and the signal has sounded. As long as the pump is silent we know that it is not full, but that little signal and the accompanying steam running from the open tap are as good as a telegram from the distant roof. So we can always tell in the Church of God when it is not full. There are some Christians whose bell only rings once in a very long time and whose over-flow is so feeble and infrequent that it would scarcely furnish one good drink to a poor thirsty wayfarer.

Beloved, let us keep pouring out more of God's blessing and see if He will not more abundantly pour in the floods of His grace. Let us be very practical about this. Every blessing that we have received from God is a sacred trust and it will be continued only as we use it for Him. Our salvation is not our own; it belongs to every perishing soul on the face of the globe who has not yet had the opportunity of accepting Jesus. Our sanctification and our great secret of the fullness of Jesus is a sacred trust for every Christian who has not yet received the fullness of God, and if we do not let this light shine, it will surely become obscure and we will not be able to tell out the story of our blessing. Our healing belongs to some sufferer. Our every experience is adjusted to some heart, and will enable us to meet some brother's need if we are but faithful to the opportunities of God's providence. Oh, how clear a truth becomes to us when we are trying to tell it to others! Oh, how real the baptism of the Holy Ghost when we are kneeling by another's side to claim it for them! Oh, how the streams of Christ's healing flow through our very flesh as we are leading some poor sufferer into the truth! Oh, how the joy of our salvation swells as we see it spring in the heart that we have just led to the fountain! Oh, the fullness that God is longing to share with every vessel that has room to receive it and readiness to give? As we have therefore received His fullness let us pass it on, drinking as the living waters flow through our hands, until we shall realize in some measure, the largeness and blessedness of the great promise of the Lord, "If any man thirst, let him come unto me, and drink. He that believeth on me, as the scripture hath said, out of his belly shall flow rivers of living water."

IV

The Larger Life

"Be ye also enlarged" [2 Cor. 6:13].

THE law of growth is a fundamental principle of all nature and redemption. Whatever ceases to grow begins to die; stagnancy brings corruption; the corpse belongs to the worm; a self-contained pool becomes a malarious swamp. Vegetation springs from a seed, the seed grows into a tree, and the tree into a forest. Human life commences in infancy and develops to maturity. The word of God has all unfolded from a single promise. The great plan of redemption has been a ceaseless progression, and will be through the ages upon ages that are yet to come.

The experience of the soul is a growth. True, it must have a starting point. We cannot grow into Christianity; we must be born from above and then grow. And so sanctification is progressive, and yet it has a definite beginning. Christ is completely formed within us, but He is the infant Christ, and grows up to the maturity of the perfect man in us just as He did in His earthly life.

It is here that the enlargement of our text meets us. It is only the truly consecrated Christian that grows. The other treads the ceaseless circle of the wilderness. But he has crossed the Jordan and begun the conquest of the land and the progressive experience of which it was the beautiful pattern and symbol. No book in the Bible has more progress in it than the book of Joshua, and yet from the very beginning it is the life of one who has wholly died to self and sin and has taken Christ for full salvation and is walking in the heavenly places in Him.

And even the book of Joshua only begins its highest

advance when it is almost ended. It is after the whole land is subdued, that the call comes, "How long are ye slack to go to possess the land? . . . There remaineth yet very much land to be possessed." And then it is that old Caleb, who has the weight of eighty-four years on his honored head, steps forth and claims the privilege of entering upon the boldest and hardest campaign of his life, the conquest of Hebron and the Anakim. It is to us then, who know the Lord Jesus in His fullness, that He is saying, "Be ye also enlarged."

I. WHAT IT MEANS TO BE ENLARGED

1. We need a larger vision. All great movements begin in great ideas. There is no progress without a new thought as its embryo. China has remained the same for three thousand years because China has not accepted a new idea. Her teacher is a man who lived long before Christ, and for nearly thirty centuries she has followed the ideas of Confucius and is just the same today as she was thirty centuries ago. Let China receive the American idea or the Christian idea and she will be revolutionized at once.

So the first step in our advance must be a new conception of the truth as it is in Jesus and a larger view of His word and will for us. We do not need a new Bible, but we need new eyes to read our Bible and brighter light to shine upon its deep and pregnant pages. We need to see, not simply a system of exegesis or a system of Biblical exposition and criticism; a thorough knowledge of the letter and its wondrous framework of history, geography, antiquities and ancient languages; but a vivid, large and spiritual conception of what it means for us and what God's thought in it for each of us is. We want to take it as the message of heaven to the twentieth century and our generation, nay, the living voice of the

Son of God to us this very hour, and to see in it the very idea which He Himself has for our life and work; to take in the promises as He understands them, the commandments as He intends them to be obeyed, and the hopes of the future as He unfolds them upon the near horizon of their approaching fulfillment. How little have we grasped the length and breadth and depth and height of this heavenly message! How little have we realized its authority and its personal directness to us! "Open thou mine eyes, that I may behold wondrous things out of thy law!" "I will run in the way of thy commandments, when thou shalt enlarge my heart." That ye may be filled with "the spirit of wisdom and revelation in the knowledge of him: the eyes of your understanding being enlightened; that ye may know what is the hope of his calling, and what the riches of the glory of his inheritance in the saints." May the Lord grant it to each of us in the largest possible measure in accordance with His will!

2. We need a larger faith. What is the use of light if we do not use it? We need a faith that will personally appropriate all that we understand, and a faith so large that it will reach the fullness of God's great promises; so large that it will rise to the level of each emergency as it comes into our life. Do we not often feel that a promise has been brought to us with a light and power that we have been unable to claim and a need has arisen that we are persuaded God is able to meet, but for which we are conscious our faith is not grasping the victory, at least according to the full measure of the exigency? This ought not so to be. If all things are possible to him that believeth we ought to have all things in His will for every moment of life's need. The divine pattern of faith is the faith of God. Oh, let us be enlarged to this high measure!

3. We need a larger love. We need a love that will meet God's claim of perfect love, as He has said, "Thou

shalt love the Lord thy God with all thy heart, and with all thy soul, and with all thy mind." We need a love that will love one another "even as he has loved us." We need a love that will love our enemies and pray for them that despitefully use us and persecute us. We need a love that will love the lost as He loves them, overcoming our repugnance to every personal condition, and delighting to suffer or sacrifice for their salvation with the joy that counts it no sacrifice. We need a love that will take our brother's need and pain as if it were our own, and "remember those in bonds as bound with them, and them that suffer adversity as being also in the body." We need that love of which Paul writes, "Charity suffereth long, and is kind; charity envieth not; charity vaunteth not itself, is not puffed up, doth not behave itself unseemly, seeketh not her own, is not easily provoked, thinketh no evil; rejoiceth not in iniquity, but rejoiceth in the truth; beareth all things, believeth all things, hopeth all things, endureth all things."

4. We need a larger joy. We need a joy that will not only rejoice in the gifts of God, but will rejoice in God Himself and find in Him our portion and our boundless and everlasting delight. We need a joy that will not only rejoice in the sunshine but in the hour of darkness and apparent desertion, when men misunderstand us, when circumstances are against us and when even God seems to have forgotten us. We need a joy that will not only rejoice in all things, but rejoice evermore. We need a joy that even when we do not feel the joy, will "count it all joy," and rejoice by faith. We need a joy so large, so deep, so divine that it will not feel its sacrifices, will not talk about its trials, but will "endure the cross despising the shame," "for the joy set before us."

5. We need a larger experience. We do not mean by this any mere state of emotional feeling, but a larger

range of Christian living, a bringing of Christ more into everything; an experience that will prove Him in all situations, amid secular business, exasperating circumstances, baffling perplexities, extreme vicissitudes; and, going all round the circle of human life, will be able to say, "Not that I speak in respect of want: for I have learned, in whatsoever state I am, therewith to be content. I know both how to be abased, and I know how to abound: everywhere and in all things I am instructed both to be full and to be hungry, both to abound and to suffer need. I can do all things through Christ which strengtheneth me." That is a large experience. That is a degree in the school of Christ that will out-weigh all the D.D.'s of all the colleges.

6. We need a larger work. We do not mean by this that we need a larger sphere. That may not be. That certainly is not the case if we are not filling our present; but we need a better quality of work. We need to finish our unfinished work. We need to do the things that we have thought of doing, intended to do, talked about doing, and are abundantly able to do. We need to do the work that can be done in the intervals and interstices of life, the work that can be done on the way and on the wing, *between* times as well as *in* times of special service and appointment; the word that can be spoken as we casually meet people; the work that can be done by the wayside and on the crossroads of life, where souls meet that never meet again. Sometimes the ministry that can be performed at such a moment becomes the pivot for hundreds of souls and eternal ages to turn upon. We need a work that is larger in its *upward* direction, more wholly for God, more singly devoted to His glory, and more satisfied with His approval whether men are pleased or not. And we need a larger conception and realization of the work that He expects of us in the special line in which He has

been developing our Christian life. Most of those who read these lines or hear these words have been called to know Christ in a measure unknown to the great mass of the people of God, and we have not yet realized what God expects of us in spreading these special truths and extending this blessed movement, of which Christ is the centre and substance, over all the land and over all the world. God is calling us at this time to a larger faith for this special work—the testimony of Jesus in all His fullness to all the world.

7. We need a larger hope. We need to realize more vividly, more personally, more definitely, what the coming of the Lord means, and means to us, until the future shall become alive with the actual expectation and ever immanent prospect of His Kingdom and His reward. Oh how little this great hope has been to the hearts and lives of most of us until within a few years! How utterly blind the majority of Christians are to it as an actual experience! How much inspiration is it fitted to lend to the heart that truly realizes it! May the Lord enlarge our hopes and intensify them until this becomes, next to the love of Jesus, the most inspiring, stimulating, quickening motive of our Christian life and work!

8. We need a larger baptism of the Holy Spirit, for this is the true summing up of all we have said. It is one thing, not many things, that we need; and, filled with the Spirit in still larger measure, the fruit of the Spirit shall expand and increase in proportion. We need more room for His indwelling, more scope for His expanding, more channels for His outflow. We are not straitened in Him, we are straitened in ourselves. "He giveth not the Spirit by measure," but we receive Him in very confined and small capacities. He wants more room; He wants our entire being, and He wants so to fill it that we shall be

expanded into larger possibilities for His inworking and His outflowing.

Beloved, "be ye enlarged." And not only in all these senses and directions, which, no doubt, have searched us and made us realize the limitations of our present lives, but we want to be enlarged in the quality of our life; we want not only more breadth and length, but we want depth and height, a more spiritual, a more mellow, a more mature fruition, and a more established, settled and immovable standing in and for Him.

II. CONSIDERATIONS AND DIRECTIONS WITH A VIEW TO OUR ENLARGEMENT

1. In order to our being enlarged we must be delivered from and lifted above our old conceptions, ideas and experiences. In a word, we must be delivered from our past. Old things must pass away before all things can be made new. We must die to our religious self as well as to our sinful self. It was when he was far on in the spiritual life that Paul uttered the sublime aspiration, "Forgetting those things which are behind, and reaching forth unto those things which are before, I press towards the mark for the prize of the high calling of God in Christ Jesus." In the strata of our globe we find traces of the wreck of former conditions of organic life. There was a creation and then there was a disintegration, and on its ruins a new and higher development. So in the spiritual world, we come to the place where we are conscious that the old experience fails to satisfy. The old "Rephidims" are dry and we must open some new rock of Horeb and receive supplies from a higher source than before. When you find your old nest ceasing to rest you, be willing to leave it, and like the eaglets, be hurled into space, that you may be taught to fly. Let the old things pass away. They are but the basis of something better.

Let the old turn-pike be broken up. The King's Highway is to be built above it, and God's great elevated railway carry us where formerly we trod with weary feet.

There is nothing that keeps us from advancement more than ruts and drifts, wheel-tracks into which our chariots roll and then move on in the narrow line with unchanging monotony, currents in life's stream on which we are borne in the old direction until the law of habit almost makes advance impossible. The true remedy for all this is to commence each day anew and to commence at nothing; taking Christ afresh to be the Alpha and Omega for a deeper, higher, diviner experience, waiting even for His conception of thought, desire, prayer, and afraid lest our highest thought should be below His great plan of wisdom and love.

Are there not some of us, beloved, who have been trying a good while to get back an old experience? If we succeeded we should only be where we were, and if we are only going to get where we were, we have abandoned the law of progress and begun the downward retrogression. God has Himself withered by His own consuming breath the flower and fragrance of your former joys, that He may lead you into something better. Let your old experience go, and take the living, everlasting Christ instead. Be willing to be enlarged according to His thought, and exceeding abundantly above all that you have yet been able to ask or think.

2. If we would be enlarged according to the thought of God, we must be delivered from all human standards, opinions and patterns, and accept nothing less than God's own divine ideal. Multitudes are kept from spiritual progress by cast-iron systems of doctrine which have settled forever the fact that holiness is impossible in the present life, and that "no mere man, since the fall, is able to keep the commandments of God, but doth daily

break them in word, thought and deed." And then a row of human characters is set before us to prove the impossibility of sanctification, and to show the satisfying and humbling influence of human imperfection. Multitudes have made up their minds in advance that they never can have the fullness of Jesus beyond certain narrow limits, and, of course, they cannot advance beyond their standards. Now we quite agree with the statement that no mere man can be holy or blameless, but the Lord Jesus is no mere man, and when He owns and keeps the heart it is a divine holiness and a divine keeping; and we do assert that what no mere can can do, the living Christ can do and does do for those who abide in Him. Let us ake the divine measure, whatever man may think or say.

Many also are ever looking to some human example, and, "measuring themselves by themselves and comparing themselves among themselves, are not wise." Either we shall find ourselves as good as somebody else and be content, or we shall be satisfied to be as some human ideal, and so shall stop short of the only perfect pattern. We shall never grow up to the measure of the Lord until we take the Lord's own word and character as our standard and ideal; until we take our stand upon the sure and immutable ground that He who commands holiness expects us to be holy, and that He who promises His own grace and all-sufficiency to enable us to meet His demands, will not excuse us if we fail. He has offered us Himself as the life and power of our obedience and holiness, and nothing less than His own perfect example should ever satisfy our holy ambition. Looking unto Him and pressing ever closer to His side and foot-prints, we shall be transformed into the same image, from glory to glory, and shall thus go from strength to strength.

3. If we would be enlarged we must accept all that God sends us as His own divinely appointed means of

developing and expanding our spiritual life. We are so content to abide on the old plane that God has often to compel us to rise to a higher level by bringing us face to face with situations which we cannot meet without greatly enlarged measures of His grace. To use a suggestive figure, He has to send the tidal wave to flood the lowlands where we dwell that we may be compelled to move to the hills beyond; or, to take a more scriptural and beautiful figure, like the mother bird, He has to break up our downy nest and to hurl us into empty space, where we must either learn to use an entirely new and higher method of support or sink into destruction. Thus He allowed the crisis of His terrible peril to close around Jacob on the night when he bowed at Peniel in supplication, in order to bring him to the place where he could take hold of God as he never would have done; and forth from that narrow pass of peril Jacob came enlarged in his faith and knowledge of God, and in the power of a new and victorious life. He had to suffer Israel to be shut in at the Red Sea that they might be compelled to take hold of God for their supernatural help, or perish. He had to compel David, by a long and painful discipline of years, to learn the almighty power and faithfulness of his God, and to grow up into the established principles of faith and godliness, which were indispensable for his subsequent and glorious career as the king of Israel. Nothing but the extremities in which Paul was constantly placed could ever have taught him, and taught the church through him, the full meaning of the great promise he so learned to claim, "My grace is sufficient for thee." And nothing but our trials and perils would ever have led some of us to know Him as we do, to trust Him as we have, and to draw from Him the measures of grace which our very extremities made indispensable.

Often He calls us to a work far beyond our natural

strength or endowments, but the emergency only throws us upon Him, and we always find Him equal to the need which His wisdom and providence have brought in our way. It is said that good Mrs. Booth, the great associate leader of the Salvation Army, and perhaps the most gifted Christian woman in England, was led into all her public work by being compelled unexpectedly to face a large congregation and fill an appointment of which she had not dreamed. Two courses were open,—one to shrink and evade the unexpected issue, the other to throw herself upon God for larger resources of wisdom, utterance and power. She was astonished at the answer which her Father gave as she went forward in simple confidence, and from that hour she dwelt in the large place of divine sufficiency and world-wide usefulness, into which she had almost been forced.

Many of us can remember how in the beginning of our Christian work we ventured to accept positions of responsibility for which we felt we were inadequate, but, as we threw ourselves upon God and dared to go forward, His grace was sufficient. When a young minister of twenty-one, and just leaving my theological seminary, I had the choice of two fields of labor,—one an extremely easy one, in a delightful town with a refined, affectionate and prosperous church, just large enough to be an ideal field for one who wished to spend a few years in quiet preparation for future usefulness; the other, a large, absorbing city church, with many hundred members, and overwhelming and heavy burdens, which were sure to demand the utmost possible care, labor and responsibility. All my friends, teachers and counsellors advised me to take the easier place. But an impulse, which I now believe to have been, at least indirectly, from God, even though there must have been some human ambition in it, led me to feel that if I took the easier place I should probably rise to meet it and no more, and if I took the harder I should not rest short of all its requirements. I found it even so. My early ministry was developed and the habit of venturing on difficult undertakings was largely established, by the grace of God, through the necessities of this difficult position.

Let us then, beloved, be willing to be enlarged, although it may involve many a sacrifice, many a peril, many a hazardous undertaking.

4. If we would be enlarged let us take the Holy Ghost Himself to enlarge us by filling us with His fullness. The highest enlargement is by the power of expansion. It is the incoming wave which enlarges the little pool as it fills it, and then rolls back to the sea to return with still larger fullness and make yet ampler room. Nothing so sweeps away the littleness of our conceptions of God, the pettiness of our faith, the narrowness of our love, the meanness of our self-consciousness, the insignificance of our work, as to be filled with His glorious presence, to look in His face, to feel the tides of His love, and to be thrilled with the touch of His own heart and its mighty thoughts and purposes for us and for the world for which He died. We need not say that the place to receive Him is the mercy seat. Waiting before Him in prayer, receiving Him in communion, drinking deeper and deeper of His life and love, the vessel is not only filled but expanded, until we know something of the prayer of the apostle in the third chapter of Ephesians, "That he would grant you, according to the riches of his glory, to be strengthened with might by his Spirit in the inner man; that Christ may dwell in your hearts by faith; that ye, being rooted and grounded in love, may be able to comprehend with all saints what is the breadth, and length, and depth, and height, and to know the love of Christ, which passeth

knowledge, that ye might be filled with all the fulness of God."

5. If we would be enlarged to the full measure of God's purpose, let us endeavor to realize something of our own capacities for His filling. We little know the size of the human soul and spirit. Never, until He renews, cleanses and enters the heart can we have any adequate conception of the possibilities of the being whom God made in His very image, and whom He now renews after the pattern of the Lord Jesus Himself. When we remember that God has made the human soul to be His temple and abode, and that He knows how to make the house that can hold His infinite fullness, we may be very sure that there are capacities in the human spirit which none of us have ever yet begun to realize. We know something of them as all our nature quickens into spring-tide life at the coming of the Holy Spirit, and as from time to time new baptisms awaken the dormant powers and susceptibilities that we did not know we possessed.

But all this is but the beginning of an infinite possibility. Oh, how He has sometimes taken a low, coarse, brutal nature, that for years has seemed to possess no capacity except for crime and sensuality, and made it not only as pure but as bright as an angel's mind, and brought forth from that brain, that voice, that tongue, that taste, that imagination, when illuminated and vivified by the Holy Ghost, such glorious fruitions as the life work of a Harry Moorhouse, the eloquence of a Richard Weaver, the marvelous allegory of a John Bunyan, and the exquisite hymns and poems of a Newton.

Oh let us give Him the right to make the best of us, and, with wonder filled, we shall some day behold the glorious temple which He has reared, and shall say, "Lord, what is man that thou hast set thine heart upon him?"

6. If we would rise to the full measure of God's

standard for us, let us realize the magnitude of God as well as of our own being, for it is with nothing less than Himself that He means to fill us. Let us take in the full dimensions of His resources of grace, their length, their breadth, their depth, their height; and then let us measure, if we can, the magnitude of God who is the living substance and personal source of all this grace, and we shall have some approximation at least to what the apostle means when he exclaims, "Now unto him that is able to do exceeding abundantly above all that we ask or think, according to the power that worketh in us, unto him be glory in the church by Christ Jesus, throughout all ages world without end. Amen."

7. And, finally, let us remember that we have eternal years in which to develop all this divine ideal. Oh, could we see ourselves as we shall some day be, could we behold this morning that glorious creature that the universe shall some day come to behold in the image of the Son of God, could we see our faces shining as the sun in the kingdom of our Father, and hear the songs of rapture that will yet burst from our lips in higher notes than angels ever sung, we would wonder at the littleness of our faith today and our fear to ask our Father for the merest fraction in advance of our great inheritance.

This is no picture of the imagination. This is no soaring dream of hope or fancy, for He has told us that we shall be like Him when He shall appear. Oh, could we take you up to heaven this morning and let you gaze a single moment on the face of Jesus, shining "as the sun shineth in his strength"; could we comprehend the infinite wisdom that this very moment is taking in the whole sweep of the universe in the grasp of His thought, listening to a thousand prayers at once, administering the government of innumerable worlds, and yet at leisure to listen to our faintest cry; could we measure His omnipotence as He holds in His hands the reins of universal power and dominion; could we stand the vision of His beauty and feel the thrill of His love in all its ecstatic power, we would have some conception of what we are ourselves yet to be: for "we shall know even as we are known"; we shall share the work of His omnipotence; we shall shine in all His beauty; we shall reflect His moral perfections; we shall sit with Him upon His throne; we shall be invested with His transcendent glory; and all we receive of Him today is a mere installment in advance of that which is already our own by right of inheritance, and which shall be actually realized as fast as we can take it in. We have eternity before us. Beloved, let us rise to the height of such a prospect even here; let us walk as those who dwell in heavenly places and share the resurrection and ascension life of their living Head.

Rise with thy risen Lord,
  Ascend with Christ above,
And in the heavenlies walk with Him
  Whom seeing not, you love.

Look on your trials here,
  As He beholds them now,
Look on this world as it will seem
  When glory crowns your brow.

Walk as a heavenly race,
  Princes of royal blood;
Walk as the children of the Lord,
  The sons and heirs of God.

Fear not to take your place
  With Jesus on the throne,
  And bid the pow'rs of earth and hell
  His sovereign sceptre own.

Your full redemption rights
  With holy boldness claim,
And to its utmost fullness prove
  The power of Jesus' name.

Your life is hidden now,
  Your glory none can see,
But when He comes, His bride will shine
  All glorious as He.

V

The Death of Self

"Not I, but Christ" [Gal. 2:20].

THE story of Abraham, Ishmael and Isaac is a parable, illustrating this text. The casting out of Ishmael is most clearly declared in this very epistle to be an allegory setting forth the spiritual experience of the believer when he dies to the law and sin through the cross of Jesus Christ, and comes into the resurrection life of his Risen Lord. But there is something more than the experience of Ishmael and our deliverance from the power of indwelling sin. In the patriarchal story, this was followed by the offering up of Isaac on Mount Moriah, and there can be no doubt that this sets forth the deeper spiritual experience into which the fully consecrated heart must come, when even the sanctified self is laid upon the altar like Isaac upon the mount and we become dead henceforth, not only to sin, but to that which is worse than sin, even self.

There is a foe whose hidden power
The Christian well may fear;
More subtle far than inbred sin,
And to the heart more dear.
It is the power of selfishness,
The proud and wilful I;
And e'er my Lord can live in me,
My very self must die.

This is the lesson of Isaac's offering and Paul's experience. "I have been crucified with Christ," that is the death of sin; "nevertheless I live," that is the new life in the power of His resurrection; "Yet not I, but Christ liveth in me," that is the offering of Isaac, the deliverance from self, and the substitution of Christ Himself for even the new self; a substitution so complete that even the faith by which this life is maintained is no longer our self-sustained confidence but the very "faith of the Son of God who loved me and gave himself for me," that is, instead of me, and as my Substitute.

I. The Forms of Self

We read in the book of Joshua of the three sons of Anak, who formed the Anakim, the race of giants who held the city of Hebron before Caleb's conquest, and were the terror of the Israelites. Literally Anak means long-necked, and represents pride, confidence, wilfulness, and self-sufficiency. The first of the Anakim may be called,

1. Self-will, the disposition to rule, and especially to rule ourselves; the spirit that brooks no other will and is its own law and god. Therefore the first step in the consecrated life is unconditional surrender. This is indispensable to break the power of self at the centre, and to establish forever the absolute sovereignty of the will of God in the heart and life of the Christian. We cannot abide in holiness and we cannot be wholly used for God until self-will is so utterly crucified that we could not even think for an instant of acting contrary to His will or without His orders. This is obedience, and obedience is the law of the Christian life and must be absolute, unquestioning, and without any possible exception. "Ye are my friends, if ye do whatsoever I command you."

It is true that God requires of us in the life of faith the exercise of a very strong will continually, and there is no doubt that faith itself is largely the exercise of a sanctified and intensified will, but in order to do this it is necessary that our will be wholly renounced and God's will invariably accepted instead, and then we can put into it all the strength and force of our being, and will it even as God wills it, and because He wills it. In short, it is an exchanged will; the despotic tyranny of Anak exchanged for the wise, beneficent yet still more absolute sovereignty of God.

2. Self-confidence is the next of Anak's race. It is the spirit that draws its strength from self alone and disdains the arm of God and the help of His grace. In a milder form it is the spirit that trusts its own spiritual graces or virtues, its morality perhaps, its courage, its faith, its purity, its steadfastness, its joy, and its transitory emotions of hope, enthusiasm, or zeal. It is just as necessary to die to our self-sufficiency as to our self-will. If we do not we shall have many a fall and failure until we learn, with the most triumphant and successful laborer that ever followed the footsteps of his Lord, that "we are not sufficient of ourselves to think anything as of ourselves, but our sufficiency is of God." The sanctified heart is not a self-constituted engine of power, but is just a set of wheels and pulleys that are absolutely dependent upon the great central engine whose force is necessary continually to move them. It is just a capacity to hold God; just a vessel to be filled with His goodness, held and used by His hand; just a possibility of which He, in His abiding life is constantly the motive power and impelling force. The word "consecrate" in Hebrew means "to fill the hand," and beautifully suggests the idea of an empty hand which God Himself must continually fill.

3. Self-glorying is the last and most impious of these Canaanitish tribes. He takes the very throne of Jehovah and claims the glory due unto Him alone. Sometimes it is a desire for human praise. Sometimes it is more subtle, the pride so proud that it will not stoop to care for the approval of others, and its supreme delight is in its own self-consciousness and superiority, ability or goodness. Metaphysicians have sometimes made this happy

distinction, that vanity is an inferior vice to pride. Vanity only seeks the praise of others but pride disdains the opinions of others and rests back in the complacent consciousness of its own excellency. Whatever its phase may be, the root and principle is the same. It is impious self, sitting on the throne of God, and claiming the honor and glory that belong to Him alone.

These three forms of self are illustrated by three very solemn examples in the word of God. Saul the first king of Israel is a fearful monument of the peril of self-will. His downward career began in a single act of disobedience, a disobedience which seemed to have respect to a mere question of detail, but which was really an act of self-will, a substitution of his choice for God's express command. The prophet Samuel characterizes his sin in these very expressive words, "To obey is better than sacrifice, and to hearken than the fat of rams. For rebellion is as the sin of witchcraft, and stubbornness is as iniquity and idolatry. Because thou hast rejected the word of the Lord, he hath also rejected thee from being king." It is evident from these words that the very essence of Saul's sin lay in this element of willfulness and stubbornness which had dared to substitute his own ideas and preferences for the word of Jehovah. From this moment his obedience was necessarily qualified, and of course worthless, and God sent His prophet to choose another king, who, although full of human imperfections, had this one thing on which God could fully depend, namely, a purpose to obey God when he fully understood His will. Therefore God calls David "a man after my own heart, who shall perform all my will." David made many mistakes and committed many dark and terrible sins, but they were when under strong temptation and when blinded by passion and haste, but never with the purpose of disobeying God, or, at the time, with the consciousness that he was transgressing. The sad, sad story of Saul's downward descent and final and tragic ruin should be enough to make us tremble at the peril which lies before the willful soul, and to lead us to cry, "Not my will, but thine be done."

We have just as marked an instance of the peril of self-confidence in Simon Peter. Strong in his transitory enthusiasm, and ignorant of the real weakness of his own heart, he honestly meant what he said, when he exclaimed, "Though all men should deny thee yet will I never deny thee." But alas! The shameful denial, the upbraiding look of Jesus, the bitter tears of penitence and the sad days of the crucifixion that followed had to teach him the lesson of his nothingness, and the necessity of walking henceforth with downward head in the strength of the Lord alone.

We are not left without as vivid and impressive an object lesson of the last form of self-will—the pride that glories in its own achievements or excellencies. "Is not this great Babylon that I have built?" cries Nebuchadnezzar, in the hour of his triumph, as he looks upon that splendid city, which was indeed a paragon of human glory, and surveys in his imagination the mightier empire of which it was the metropolis, an empire which literally comprised the world. If mortal could ever have cause to glory in earthly magnificence, Nebuchadnezzar had, for God Himself had compared him and his kingdom to a majestic head of gold and had symbolized his power under the figure of a winged lion, combining the majesty and sovereignty of the eagle and the lion in one splendid image. But the very instant that vain-glorious word reached the ears of God, the answer fell from heaven like a knell of judgment, "The kingdom is departed from thee. And they shall drive thee from men, and thy dwelling shall be with the beasts of the field, . . . till thou know that the most High ruleth in the kingdom of men, and giveth it to whomsoever he will." This is the glorying of the carnal heart, but even the follower of God may mingle his own self-seeking and his own honor with his work for God and thus impair his usefulness and lose his own recompense.

There is not a more pitiful picture in the long panorama of the Bible than that morbid and grumbling prophet, sitting outside the gates of Nineveh under a withered gourd, his face blistered and swollen with the scorching sun and his eyes red with useless weeping; asking God that he might die, because his ministry had been dishonored; and presenting a spectacle of ridiculous melancholy and chagrin while all around him millions were rejoicing and praising God for the mercy which had just delivered them from an awful catastrophe. Poor Jonah! God had given him the most honorable ministry ever yet accorded to a human being. He was the first foreign missionary. He had been sent to preach to the mightiest empire on the face of the globe and the imperial city of the world, proud Nineveh! His preaching had been successful as no mortal ever had succeeded. The whole city was lying prostrate on their faces at the footstool of mercy in penitence and prayer through his words, and the nation's heart, for a moment at least, was turned to God. And yet so full of himself had all his work been, so utterly was he absorbed in his own credit, reputation and honor, that when God listened to the penitent cries of the Ninevites and revoked the sentence which Jonah himself had uttered, and rendered his prophecy null and void, so that instead of his word coming to pass, he himself would probably be afterwards ridiculed as a fanatic and idle alarmist, poor Jonah became disgusted and exasperated and like a petted child went out and threw himself upon his face on the ground and asked God to kill him, just because He had by His mercy spoiled his reputation as a true prophet. He could not see, as God did, the unspeakable horror and anguish that had been averted. He could not see the joy of the divine heart in exercising mercy and in hearing the penitent cries of the people. He could not see the great principle of grace which underlies the divine threatenings. He could not see that great-souled pity, that felt for the one hundred and twenty thousand infant children of the great capital, or the dumb brutes, which would have moaned in their dying agony, if Nineveh had fallen.

All he could see was Jonah's reputation as a true prophet or what people might say when they found that his word had not come to pass; and with that one little worm gnawing at the root, his peace and happiness, like his own gourd, withered away and God had to set him up as a sort of dried specimen of selfishness, to show the meanness and misery of the self-life that mingles its own glory with the sacred work of the glorious God, and which, ever since the days of Jonah, has rendered it impossible for God to use many a gifted man, and has blighted the church of Christ and rendered vain the ministry of thousands because God could not use them without giving to men the glory which He will never give to another. God had tried to kill Jonah before He sent him to Nineveh, for He knew the secret bane of his heart and, so He immersed him for three days and nights in the sea and buried him in the bowels of a whale; but out of that Jonah came, as a great many other people come out of the experience of sanctification, with a big self, supreme even in the sin-cleansed soul. Oh let us lift up the heart-felt prayer,

> **O to be saved from myself, dear Lord,**
> **O to be lost in Thee!**
> **O that it may be no more I,**
> **But Christ that lives in me!**

II. THE EFFECTS OF SELF

1. It dishonors God and sets up a rival on His throne. The devil was not altogether a liar when he said to our first parents, "Ye shall be as gods." This is just what fallen man tries to be, a god unto himself. This is the essence of the sin of selfishness, that it puts man in the place of God by making him a law and an end unto himself. Whenever any person acts, either because it is his own selfish will, or for his own self-interest, purely as an end, he is claiming to be his own god and directly disobeying the first commandment, "Thou shalt have no other gods before me." Moreover, in assuming the place of God, he is doing it in a spirit of the very opposite of God's, for God is love, and love is the very opposite of selfishness. He is thus mimicking God and proving, at the same time, his utter unfitness to occupy His throne by his unlikeness to Him.

2. It leads to every other sin and brings back the whole power of the carnal nature. For while self alone attempts to keep the heart, it finds sin and Satan too strong. A self-perfection is not possible for any man. There must be more than "I" before there can be victory. In the seventh of Romans the apostle tells us what "I, myself" can do and that is, ineffectually struggle. In the eighth it is what "Christ in me" can do, and that is victory and everlasting love. The man or woman who only goes so far as to receive Adamic purity, if such a thing be included in the Gospel at all, will soon have the next chapter of Adamic history, and that is the temptation and fall. But the man who receives Christ to dwell within and keep the heart by His mighty power, shall rise "to the measure of the stature of the fulness of Christ."

3. The self-life leads back to the dominion of Satan. Satan's own fall began probably in a form of self-love.

Made to be dependent on God every moment, probably he became independent; and contemplating his own perfection, and thinking it was something that was his own, he became separated from God, and then inevitably fell into rebellion against Him and eternal rivalry, disobedience and all that can be the opposite of the divine and the holy. And so still, any soul that becomes self-constituted or occupied with its own virtues, and tries to be independent of Jesus, either as the source of its strength or the supreme end of its being, will fall under the power of Satan and share his awful descent. Where can we find a sadder illustration of the end of self than in the story of Saul? He began with Saul and ended with Satan. The first chapter is self-will, the last is the awful night at Endor and the bloody day of death and ruin on Mount Gilboa.

4. It is fatal to the spirit of love and harmony. It is the opposite of love and the source of strife, bigotry, suspicion, sectarianism, envy, jealousy and the whole race of social sins and grievances that afflict the Christian life and the church of God. It is the mother of the strifes and sectarianisms of the church from the very beginning. Where it prevails there can be no true unity, no happy co-operation. You never can have a harmonious church or a happy family where self is predominant in the hearts of the people. The very secret of Christian co-operation and happy church life is "forbearing one another in love," endeavoring to keep the unity of the Spirit in the bond of peace, "in honor preferring one another."

5. It mars our work for God. Self-will will try to force the chariots of God's power and grace upon our own side-tracks and that God will never permit. Self-confidence will seek to build up the kingdom of Christ by human means and unsanctified instrumentalities, and presume to go where God has not sent and to do what God

has not qualified us by His Holy Spirit to do. The result is, it is but crude work, defiled by worldliness and sin, impermanent and unfruitful, as much of the Christian work of today is, in all the churches of Christ. And above all others, the spirit of self-glorying will try to use the pulpit, the organ gallery, the subscription books, the religious paper, the charitable scheme, the very mission for winning souls, as a channel for developing some brilliant character, or to glorify some rich man or woman, or minister to the spiritual self-sufficiency of some successful worker; and God is disgusted with the spirit of idolatry, and His Holy Spirit turns away grieved for the honor of Jesus. Until we are so yielded to our Master that He and He alone can be glorified in our work, the Lord cannot trust us with much service for Him or it will simply become the pinnacle of the temple from which the devil will hurl us down.

6. Self makes us unhappy. It is a root of bitterness in every heart where it reigns. The secret of joy is hidden in the bosom of love, and the arms of self are too short ever to reach it. Not until we dwell in God and God in us and learn to find our happiness in being lost in Him and living for His glory and for His people, shall we ever know the sweets of divine blessedness. All the world cannot fill this hungry heart. All our spiritual treasures only corrupt if we hoard them for ourselves. Only water that runs is living water. And only when it is poured into other empty vessels does it become wine. The self-willed man is always a miserable man. He gets his own way and does not enjoy it, and wishes after he has had it, that he had never got it, for it usually leads him over a precipice. The self-sufficient man can never know the springs which lie outside his own little heart, and the self-glorying man, like poor Herod, is eaten of the worms of corruption and remorse with which God

always feeds the impious soul that dares to claim the honors due to Him alone.

7. Self-love always leads to a fall. The boasted wisdom must be proved to be foolishness. The proud arm must be laid, like Pharaoh's, in the dust. The self-sufficient boast, like Peter's, must be answered by his own failure. The disobedient path which refuses God's wise and holy will, must be proved to be a false way. Every idol must be abolished, every high thing brought low, and no flesh glory in His presence.

Oh, beloved, if you are going on in your own will, your own strength, for your own gratification and glory, beware! Thorns lie in your pathway, serpents lurk beneath your feet, yawning abysses, perilous precipices, angry tempests, midnight darkness, many a sorrow, many a tear, many a fall, await you. "He that trusteth in his own heart is a fool." "There is a way that seemeth right unto a man but the ends thereof are the ways of death."

Oh, let us ask our faithful God to save us from this tyrant that dishonors God, that leads us into captivity to Satan, that withers love, mars the work of God, poisons all our happiness, and plunges us into failure and ruin; and so to show us that we are nothing, that we shall be glad to have Christ live in us, our "all in all."

III. THE REMEDY FOR SELF

1. God often has let self have its way until it cures us effectually by showing us the misery and failure which it brings. This is the only good there is in our own struggling, that it shows us the vanity of the struggle and prepares us the more quickly to surrender to God. And so sometimes even our disobedience is overruled to make us fear to repeat the experiment or to venture again one step beyond our Father's will. Let us beware, however,

how we attempt the experiment ourselves for there is always one step too far ever to return.

2. God has placed around us the blessed restraints of other hearts and lives as checks upon our selfishness, and links, which almost compel us to reach beyond ourselves and work with and live for others. He has made no man independent of his brethren. "We are fitly framed together" and so grow into a holy temple in the Lord. We are adjusted, bone to His bone, and, by that which every joint supplieth, the body is ministered unto and groweth into the fullness of His stature. The church of Christ is no autocracy where one man can be a dictator or a judge, but a fellowship where One alone is Master. Any work which develops into a one-man despotism becomes withered. It is truth that God has ranks of workers but they are all harmonious and linked in heavenly love. The man who cannot work with his brethren in mutual comfort and harmony has something yet to learn in his own Christian life. True, God does not require us to work with unsanctified men; but there are plenty of sanctified ones, thank God, today, where any earnest heart can find a congenial fellowship of service; and while He will teach any of us by ourselves, and wants us to be independent of our brethren in the sense of leaning on them instead of God, yet He does require that we should be able to cooperate with them for God, submitting ourselves one to another in the fear of God, one sowing and another reaping, and both rejoicing together, "bearing one another's burdens and so fulfilling the law of Christ," "true yoke-fellows." And so by innumerable phrases and figures He has taught us the blessed truth of Christian cooperation in the spirit of self-renunciation and mutual confidence and love. Let us receive these blessed lessons and helps and let Him so slay in us the self-asserting "I" that we can be true yoke-

fellows, and like David's men, be able to "keep rank" in the great host of God.

3. The love of Jesus is the divinely appointed prescription for the death of self. Paul expresses it beautifully, "We thus judge, that if one died for all, then were all dead: And that he died for all, that they which live should not henceforth live unto themselves, but unto him which died for them, and rose again."

Many of us have seen at some time a young, beautiful, petted, luxurious and selfish girl, growing up surrounded with wealth, affection, admiration, adulation, until she was wholly spoiled, and became the centre of the circle in which she lived, her whole being perverted by her selfishness. But we have seen that girl years afterwards, and we would not have known her had we not traced the intermediate steps. She was now a self-denying, loving wife and mother, her whole being devoted to the happiness of that husband whose fortunes she had followed amid poverty, obscurity and separation from all her former friends; sharing his penury, toiling for his comfort, and nursing as a faithful and loving mother, the little children who had come into her arms, with the love that never wearied, that felt no task too hard, and no work too menial. What has made all the difference? What has cast out that idol, self, from its throne? Nothing but love. That man has won her heart. He has come in and taken the place that it had occupied; it is cast out and he reigns.

That is the simple story of the death of self in the Christian life. It is the love of Jesus that has excluded it, and never, until we become fascinated with His affection, and won in complete captivity to His love, shall we cease to live unto ourselves. Then, like that girl, we will follow Him anywhere. We will toil and suffer with Him. We will be content without many things that before we thought we must have, because His smile is our sunshine, His presence is our joy, His love, shed abroad in our hearts, is our heaven, and we cannot speak or think of sacrifice or suffering, our heart is so satisfied with Him.

Beloved, if you would die to self you must fall in love with Jesus and let Him become to you the personal reality of Solomon's sweet Song in which the whole heart summers into a land of Beulah and a "Hephzibah" of joy.

4. But it is not the love of Christ merely that we want; it is the living Christ Himself. Many people have touches of the love of Christ, but He is a Christ away up in heaven. The apostle speaks of something far mightier. It is Christ Himself who lives inside and who is big enough to crowd out and keep out the little "I." There is no other that can truly lift and keep the heart above the power of self but Jesus, the Mighty Lord, the stronger than the strong man armed, who taketh away his armour wherein he trusted and spoileth all his goods and then takes forever the heart that has given him its goods. Blessed Christ! He is able not only for sin, sorrow and sickness, but He is able for you and me,—able so to be our very life, that moment by moment we shall be conscious that He in us fills us with Himself and conquers the self that ruled before. The more you try to fight a self-thought the more it clings to you. The moment you turn away from it and look to Him, He fills all the consciousness and disperses everything with His own presence. Let us abide in Him and we shall find there is nothing else to do.

5. It is almost the same thing, but another way of saying it, that the baptism and indwelling of the Holy Ghost within us will deliver and keep us from the power of self. When the cloud of glory entered the tabernacle there was no room for Moses to remain; and when filled

with the heavenly presence of the blessed Spirit we are lost in God and self hides away, and like Job we can say, "Now mine eye seeth thee. Wherefore I abhor myself and repent in dust and ashes."

Beloved, these temples were reared for Him. Let Him fill them so completely that, like the oriental temple of glass in the ancient legend, the temple shall not be seen, but only the glorious sunlight, which not only shines into it, but through it, and the transparent walls are all unseen.

It is not a new, but it is an appropriate thought, that all the things that God has used have first been sacrificed. It is a sacrificed Saviour, One who emptied Himself, and made Himself of no reputation that God has so highly exalted, and given Him a name that is above every name, "that at the name of Jesus every knee should bow, of things in heaven and things in earth and things under the earth." It was a sacrificed Isaac that God made the promised seed and the progenitor of Israel's tribes. And it was on that very Mount Moriah where Isaac was sacrificed, that God afterwards reared His glorious temple. And so it is only when our Isaac is on the altar and our whole being lost in God that He can lay the deep foundations and rear the everlasting walls of the living temple of which He is the Supreme and eternal glory.

I look back today with unutterable gratitude to the lonely and sorrowful night, when, mistaken in many things, and imperfect in all, my heart's first full consecration was made, and not knowing but that it would be death in the most literal sense before the morning light, yet with unreserved surrender I first could say,

"Jesus I my cross have taken,
All to leave and follow thee;
Destitute, despised, forsaken,
Thou from hence my All shalt be."

Never perhaps has my heart known quite such a thrill of joy as when the following Sabbath morning I gave out those lines and sang them with all my heart. And if God has been pleased to make my life in any measure a little temple for His indwelling and for His glory, and if He ever shall be please to use me in my fuller measure, it has been because of that hour, and it will be still in the measure in which that hour is made the keynote of a consecrated, crucified and Christ-devoted life.

Oh, beloved, come and let Him teach you the superlative degree of joy, the joy that has learned to say not only, "My beloved is mine," but better even, "I am my Beloved's"; and we shall find as one of our dear missionaries in China used to say, "He is willing to come into the heart of every one of us and love us to death."

VI
More Than Conquerors

"Nay, in all these things we are more than conquerors through him that loved us" [Rom. 8:37].

IT IS a great thing to be a conqueror in Christian life and conflict. It is a much greater thing to be a conqueror "in all these things" which the apostle names, a perfect host of trials, troubles and foes. But what does it mean to be "more than conqueror"?

I. It means to have a decisive victory. There are some victories that cost nearly as much as defeats, and a few more such triumphs would annihilate us. There are some battles which have to be renewed again and again until we are exhausted with the ceaseless strife. Many a Christian is kept in constant warfare through lack of courage to venture on a bold and final contest and end the strife by a decisive victory. It is blessed so to die that we are dead indeed; so to yield that the last strand of the heart's reluctance is severed; so to say "no" to the enemy that he will never repeat the solicitation. There are decisive battles in the world's history, conflicts whose issues settle the future of an empire or of a world, and the soul has such battles too. God is able to give us the grace so to win in a few encounters that there shall be no doubt about the side on which the victory falls and no danger of the contest ever being renewed again. Other battles we may have and shall have, but surely it is possible for us to settle the questions that meet us, one by one, and settle them forever.

Beloved, are not some of you weakened by this indecisiveness in your views of truth, in your steps of faith, in your refusals of temptation, in your surrender to God, in your consecration to His service and your obedience to

His special call? You have been just uncertain enough to keep the question open and tempt the adversary to renew the conflict evermore. We sometimes read in God's Word after one of David's hardest conflicts, or one of Joshua's boldest triumphs, "the land had rest from war!" Thus we have rest by becoming "more than conquerors through him that loved us."

II. It is to have such a victory as will effectually break the adversary's power and not only defend us from his attacks but effectually weaken and destroy his strength. This is one of the purposes of temptation, that we may be workers together with God in destroying evil. We read of Joshua's battles that "It was of the Lord to harden their hearts, that they should come against Israel in battle, that he might destroy them utterly." It was not enough for Israel to beat them off and be saved from their attacks, but God wanted them exterminated. And so when God allows the enemy to appear in our lives it is that we may do him irreparable and eternal injury, and thus glorify God and be workers with Christ in destroying the works of the devil. For this purpose God frequently brings to light in our own lives and in our work for God, evils that were concealed, not that they might crush us, but that we might put them aside. But for their discovery and resistance they might still have remained unrevealed and some day have broken out with fatal effectiveness. But God allows them to be provoked into activity in order to challenge our resistance and lead to our aggressive and victorious advance against them. Therefore when we find anything in our own hearts and lives, or in connection with the work of our Master committed to our hands which seems to threaten our triumph or His work, let us remember that God has allowed it to confront us, that, in His name, it might be forever put aside and rendered powerless to injure or oppose again.

Beloved, are we thus fighting the good fight of faith, resisting the devil and rising up for God against them that do wickedly? Are we looking upon our adversaries and our obstacles as things that have come, not to crush us, but to be put aside and become tributary to our successes and our Master's glory? Thus shall we be "more than conquerors through him that loved us" and as the prophet beautifully expresses it, "Behold, all they that were incensed against thee shall be ashamed and confounded: they shall be as nothing; and they that strive with thee shall perish. Thou shalt seek them, and shall not find them, even them that contended with thee: they that war against thee shall be as nothing, and as a thing of naught."

III. It is to have such a victory as brings actual benefit out of the battle and makes it tributary to our own and our Master's cause. It is possible in a certain sense to take our enemies prisoners and make them fight in our ranks, or at least do the menial work of our camp. It is possible to get such good out of Satan's assaults that he shall actually become our ally without intending it and shall find with eternal chagrin that he has been doing us real service. Doubtless he thought, when he stirred up Pharaoh to murder the little children of the Hebrews that he was exterminating a race of which he was afraid. But that very act of his brought Moses into Pharaoh's house and raised up a deliverer for Israel and the destroyer of Pharaoh. Surely that was being "more than conqueror!" The devil was not only beaten but made to work in the Lord's chain-gang as a galley slave. Again he overmatched himself when he instigated Haman to build his lofty gallows and send forth the decree for Israel's extermination, for he had the misery of seeing Haman hang on those gallows and Israel delivered. So again, no doubt, he put the Hebrew children into the furnace and Daniel into the den of lions hoping to destroy the last remnant of godliness on the earth, but lo! these heroes were "more than conquerors." Not only did they escape their destroyer, but their deliverance led to the proclamation of Nebuchadnezzar, magnifying the truth of God through the entire Babylonian empire, and to the similar confession of Darius, recognizing God throughout all the confines of the still greater Persian empire. Surely Satan was more than beaten that time!

His most audacious attempt was the crucifixion of our Lord, and all hell, no doubt, held high jubilee on that dark afternoon when Jesus sank to death; but lo! the cross has become the weapon by which Satan's head is already bruised and his kingdom is yet to be exterminated. So God makes him forge the weapons of his own destruction, and hurl the thunderbolts that fall back upon his own head. So may we ever thus turn his fiercest assaults to our advantage, and to the glory of our King.

It is very interesting to look at the old frontispiece in Wycliffe's Bible, where a group of figures are gathered round a fire which is bursting through the open pages of a holy Bible. Their countenances all wear a look of consternation, and with one consent they are gathered round the fire, trying to blow it out. There are bishops and archbishops of the church of Rome, and the devil at the head of the crowd, all blowing lustily with swollen cheeks and strained countenances. But lo! the more they blow the more it burns, until at last the fierce blaze leaps up so high and out so far and wide that they are obliged to shrink back, and even Satan himself, though used to such an atmosphere, is glad to escape from its consuming flame. So let us overcome and more than overcome our spiritual foes.

The best thing they do for us often is the discipline they bring us in our spiritual life. In this way, and in this alone, do we learn to exercise victorious faith and endure hardness as good soldiers of Jesus Christ. The two things that the Christian needs most are the power to believe and the power to suffer, and these the enemy often comes to teach us. Not until we are ready to sink beneath the pressure do we often learn the secret of triumph. It was a great thing for the American nation that she had the Mexican War before she had the War of the Rebellion. It was there that her officers were trained and fitted to lead the armies of the greater struggle. So the Lord lets the devil act as drill sergeant in His army, and teach His children the use of His spiritual weapons. So we may "count it all joy when we fall into divers temptations; knowing that the trying of our faith worketh patience."

This indeed is to be "more than conqueror," to learn such lessons from the enemy as will fit us for his next assaults and prepare us to meet him without fear of defeat. There are some things that cannot easily be learned. Our spiritual senses seem to require the pressure of difficulty and suffering to awaken all their capacities and to constrain us to prove the full resources of heavenly grace. God's school of faith is always trial, and God's school of love is provocation and wrong. Instead, therefore, of murmuring against our lot and wondering why we are permitted to be so tried, let us glorify God and put our adversary to shame by wringing a blessing from Satan's hate and hell's hostility, and we shall find after a while that the enemy will be glad to let us alone for his own sake if not for ours.

IV. To be "more than conqueror" is not only to have the victory, but the spoils of victory. When Jehoshaphat's army won their great deliverance from the hordes of Moab and Ammon, it took them three days to gather all the spoils of their enemies' camps. When David captured the camp of Ziklag's destroyers he won so vast a booty that he was able to send rich presents over all Israel among his brethren. When the lepers found their way to the deserted camp of the Syrians they found such abundance that in a single hour the famine of Samaria was turned into satiety. And so our spiritual conflicts and conquests have their rich reward in the treasures recovered from the hands of the enemy. How many things there are which Satan possess which we might and should enjoy! Oh the rich delight which fills the heart when we expel the giants of ill-temper, irritation, haste, hatred, malice and envy who long have ravaged and preyed upon all the sweetness of our life. What a luxuriant land we now enter into, when we overcome these foes, and how delightfully the spoils of peace and love and sweetness and heavenly joy are enriching us in the very things where once they reigned! How rich the spoils recovered from the cruel adversary when through the name of Jesus he is driven from our body, and the suffering frame which had groaned and trembled under his oppression springs into health and freedom and yields all the fullness of its strength to the service of God and the joy of a victorious life. Oh, the rich reward that comes to the home that has been rescued from the dominancy of the devil, perhaps in the form of drunkenness in a husband and father, or of shameful lust, or sinful vanity, or empty frivolity, or heartless worldliness, or bitter strife, evil speaking and anger in some other heart, and life once more becomes a happy Eden, with love and peace enthroned by the hearth and altar of a Christian home. Oh, the rich spoils that are to come from a world rescued from the hand of its cruel usurper. How it will bloom again in beauty, fruitfulness and blessedness, and yield its riches to its benignant and rightful King and to those who dare to conquer it for Him and shall share with Him its happy Millennial sway.

God takes special delight in making that a blessing to us which has been recovered from Satan's power. The two mightiest strong holds of ancient Canaan were Hebron and Zion. The former was the seat of the Anakim, the giant chieftains of Canaan; but the brave heroic Caleb dared to challenge them in their lair, and in the strength of God was "more than conqueror" over their terrific strength, and won the heights of Hebron as his special inheritance. But not only did he receive the dear old city of Abraham as his portion and spoil, but God took peculiar delight in subsequently blessing and honoring this very place, it would seem, just because it had been snatched from the very jaws of the enemy; for Hebron was the chosen seat where David's throne was subsequently established, and where God began the kingdom of Israel which He Himself is yet to rule in the coming age of Israel's restoration.

Still more defiant was the strength of the citadel of Zion. It was the last stronghold that the Canaanites relinquished. All through the days of Joshua and his successors they succeeded in holding it; all through the centuries of the Judges, all through the days of Saul, all through the early days of even David's kingdom. The fortress was impregnable so that the haughty Canaanites told their enemies in scorn that they would only deign to garrison it with the blind and the lame and they challenged them to capture it from its feeble and crippled defenders. But David met the challenge and Moab executed it by a glorious assault and took by storm the heights of Zion from the last chieftains of Canaan. Then it was that Israel found its true metropolis and the rescued stronghold was set apart by God Himself to be the very seat of the sacred kingdom and the monument of the glorious victory which had been achieved. There it was that David reigned; there it was that Solomon in all his glory swayed his glorious sceptre; there it was that the temple rose from the adjoining heights of Moriah full in view of Zion; there it is that Jesus is coming soon to reign once more. Oh, how rich and glorious the recompense of a single victory! How different the world's history if the old Canaanites had still been permitted to hold the heights of Jebus!

Beloved, the richest treasure of your life is held by Satan. He is too shrewd to waste his strength upon what is worthless. He has put his hand upon the sweetest, dearest and most precious things of life, and whether in your heart, in your home, or in your circle of acquaintance there you may be sure is a Hebron or a Zion that God wants you to overcome, and in overcoming which you shall find the richest inheritance of your life and your eternity, and shall forever say with rejoicing, as you realize the full meaning of your victory, "more than conqueror through him that loved us."

V. "More than conquerors" means not only the spoils of war and triumph over all the assaults of our foes, but it means new territory, aggressive warfare, and positive and ever larger conquests for the glory of our Lord and the salvation of others. Merely to beat back your foes is but a small part of the great commission of the Christian soldier. He is called not only to wield the shield of faith but also the sword of the Spirit by which he moves against the conquered foe and claims new territory with each advance. We have the armor of righteousness on the right hand and on the left. The armor on the left is for defense, but the armor on the right is for aggression. We are called, not only to "withstand in the evil day," but to go forth and reclaim the world for Christ. Such conflicts meet us in our Christian work at every step, in the souls we seek to win for Jesus, in the progress of truth, the spread of the gospel, the awakening and reviving of the church of God, the elevation of Christian life and holiness, the suppression of evil in all its myriad and gigantic forms around us, the evangelization of the world and the hastening of our Master's Kingdom and Coming. Surely we should not be ever occupied in holding our own salvation. Indeed we shall hold it best by leaving it with God and pressing on to claim the salvation of others.

In the last great European war the aggressors were the victors. If Germany had waited to be attacked and simply defended herself, probably she might have failed. But with wise and prompt aggression she hurled her hosts across the Rhine and into the battlefields of France and marched from victory to victory, her recompense being not only the conquest of her enemy's country, but the security of her own as well and her citizens, from even the touch of the enemy.

This is the best way to keep the devil off our territory; keep him busy on his own, defending his kingdom from our bold attacks. Beloved, have we settled the question of our own salvation and Christian life, and are we at leisure for the battles of the Lord and thus "more than conquerors through him that loved us"?

VI. "More than conquerors" means not only to win your battle and save your territory, but to do honor to your Captain and your God, to be a credit to your cause and so to acquit yourself in the campaign that God shall be glorified. Many of our battles are fought in view of heaven alone. That is a strange picture that the apostle gives of his trials, "We are made a gazing-stock to angels and principalities." Have you not felt, beloved, in some quiet hour, in the secret of your closet, that you were going through a decisive battle which no mortal saw. Within the silent walls of your chamber an issue was being decided which would affect all eternity. The question was, should you be true to God, should you trust Him, should you obey God, or should you compromise? It was a great thing for you that you gained the victory, but it was a greater thing for your Lord. Oh how intently He watches these spectacles! How the ranks of hell and heaven look on as some David and Goliath fight alone amidst the gaze of other worlds! How your Saviour's brow flushes with shame if you betray Him, or even shrink! How the ranks of hell shout with satisfaction when you betray the slightest weakness. And how your Master smiles with glad approval and sees of the travail of His soul with satisfaction, as like some ancient hero you dare to answer, "Our God is able to deliver us, but if not we will not bow down to the graven image which thou hast set up."

Do you know, beloved, that Christ's greatest victories were alone with God and the devil? No human eye saw that victory in the wilderness, but God saw it and was glorified. Shall we stand for Him, and so stand that He can count us, as He did His ancient prophet, His very towers and fortresses behind which He can intrench Himself and His cause, and say to us, "I have made thee this day a defenced city, and an iron pillar, and brazen walls against the whole land, . . . And they shall fight against thee but they shall not prevail against thee." "Behold, I have made thy face strong against their faces, and thy forehead strong against their foreheads. As an adamant harder than flint have I made thy forehead; fear them not, neither be dismayed at their looks, though they be a rebellious house." God wants men and women today, on whom He can depend, to stand as bulwarks and battlements against the shocks of hell's artillery. Men and women of whom He can say "upon this rock have I built my church, and the gates of hell shall not prevail against it." Shall we, beloved, be not only conquerors, but trusted soldiers whom God can use as His battle-axes and His weapons of war, as His mighty iron-clads, to carry the battle to the very ships of the enemy, not fearing their hardest blows, and hurling against them the thunder-bolts of His victorious power.

VII. "More than conquerors" means not only victory but final triumph and eternal reward. How Heaven will recompense her victors some glorious day! Two cities today are struggling for the tomb of the man who was honored in this land as the leader of the victorious army that won the battle of the Rebellion. He is honored simply because he was a conqueror. How little these earthly victories will seem some day in the light of the triumph of a Stephen, a Paul, a David Livingstone, or some gentle woman or lowly man, who stood faithful to God on some quiet battlefield which decided the issues of life, perhaps the future of nations and ages.

For four things Paul expected a crown, but the first of them was because he had fought the good fight of faith. Among the special recompenses of the Day of His Appearing there is a crown, not only for the martyr, not only for the faithful minister, not only for those who love His appearing, but for "the man that endureth temptation." "Blessed is the man that endureth temptation: for when he is tried, he shall receive the crown of life, which the Lord hath promised to them that love him." There is a chance for all of you. There is a chance for you who think that you have the hardest time of any human being.

Beloved, it is but an opportunity for coronation. Will you not only triumph, but so triumph that you shall wear a crown of life in which these tears which you shed today shall flash as crystal diamonds, and these scars of battle shall be transformed into marks of eternal beauty and everlasting honor?

But mere enthusiasm or even high and glorious purpose will not accomplish this great result. It is "through him that loved us" that we must overcome. Thank God that is possible for us all! He whom Joshua saw as Captain of the Lord's Host and whom Joshua took as his Great Commander-in-chief waits to lead your battle and claim your victory too. "I have overcome for thee," He stands exclaiming by thy side. Commit thy conflict to His hands, take Him into thy heart as strength, "be strong in the Lord and the power of his might," and "put on the whole armor of God that ye may stand against the wiles of the devil." "The battle is not yours but God's." "The Lord shall fight for you and ye shall hold your peace," and when all is accomplished and the banner waves in triumph and the crown is bestowed, we shall drape our battle-flags around His throne, and lay our diadems at His feet, and cry, not the old version, "Thanks be unto God which always causeth us to triumph," but "thanks be unto God which leadeth us in triumph through Jesus Christ our Lord." "In all these things we are more than conquerors through him that loved us."

VII

Grace Abounding

"Where sin abounded, grace did much more abound" [Rom. 5:20].

WE FIND in nature a beautiful approximation to the truth declared in this verse, a sort of parable and symbol of the glory of redemption. It is this. Go into the woods and cut a wound in the side of a living tree and then go back again a few years later and see how the tree has endeavored to heal its wound and restore the breach by a very beautiful reproductive force. The notch in the trunk is all grown up again. Not, however, with the old fibres, but with far stronger materials; and you will find the grain of the wood interlaced and twisted across the old fibres in a sort of tangle, which all your efforts would frequently be found unable to cleave asunder. In fact, the healed breach is much stronger than any other part of the tree, and nature has not only made good the loss, but far more abundantly brought good out of it.

So, it is said, a broken bone heals much more strongly than the natural bone, as though nature were determined to fortify herself against a second attack, and to turn to account, in double strength, the assault made upon her.

Very beautifully is this illustrated in the formation of the pearl. A little grain of sand or a piercing thorn in the sensitive side of the pearl oyster, irritating its nerves, provokes him, not to retaliate and thus inflict upon himself a greater wound, but to throw around the intruding element a crystalline liquid and to bury it out of sight in a smooth and beautiful gem; so that out of the thorn and the wound come beauty and victory, and the value of the little mollusk is enhanced a thousand-fold by the very incident that threatened his destruction.

This is what the apostle means in a more sublime measure when he sums up his splendid antithesis between sin and salvation, Adam and Christ, the fall and the redemption, with the magnificent declaration, "where sin abounded grace did much more abound." Out of the terrible attack which the powers of darkness hurled against the world, the wisdom and grace of heaven have brought the victory which is to prove the triumph of the ages. Out of the catastrophe which threatened man's eternal destruction, God has evolved a new creation transcendently greater and more glorious than the old. Out of the ocean depths of sin, Christ has brought the Pearl of Great Price, the church, which shall shine amid the glories of eternity with a lustre reflecting His own. Let us endeavor by the help of God to realize a little more fully this elevating and transporting truth.

1. It is illustrated in the salvation of the most abondoned sinners and the grace which is often so magnified in their conversion and subsequent usefulness. God seems to love to take the worst materials for His greatest triumps. He chose a Jacob and a David in the Old Testament, both weak and wicked men in many a terrible sense and measure, to become the respective heads of the patriarchal and the kingly periods. He saved a Manasseh after half a century of bloody crimes. He took a Rahab from the slums of Jericho, to be a mother in the line of the Messiah's ancestry. And when He would choose His most illustrious apostle to found the glorious work of the gospel among the infamous Gentile races, He took "the chief of sinners." There is no doubt that Paul's calm estimate of his own wickedness, given by the inspiration of the Holy Spirit, was not exaggerated. Moral though he was, yet even his own testimony leaves sufficient evidence of the atrocity of his religious crimes. Not satisfied with insulting the name of Jesus and abetting the mur-

derers of Stephen, His faithful martyr, he devoted himself to exterminating the followers of Christ; and with a fiendish excess of cruelty he feared not to destroy their souls as well as their bodies by committing the most fearful crimes and compelling them to blaspheme the Name of Him on whom they believed. He must have known full well the awfulness of the crimes he required of them, and that although they might even be mistaken in their faith, yet to sin against their conscience by profaning the name of Christ was, to them, the height of impiety, and on his part the very extreme of refined and Satanic cruelty.

And yet he, "the chief of sinners," tells us that he obtained mercy for this very purpose, that he might become the pattern of the principle on which God was to act in the economy of grace, namely, to "show forth all long-suffering unto them that should hereafter believe on the name of Jesus Christ to life everlasting." And this does not merely mean that God will save the most guilty, but that He will take peculiar pleasure in making more of their redeemed lives just because of their former wickedness. And so Paul can say "the grace of God was exceeding abundant towards me, with faith and love which is in Christ Jesus our Lord." "Where sin abounded grace did much more abound," not only in forgiving the sins but in making the sinner a vessel of the riches of divine grace and love, and an instrument in the hands of God for greater usefulness than ever was permitted perhaps to a mortal.

So still, through all these succeeding centuries has He loved to take the thorn and the thistle and turn them into the fir tree, and the myrtle and make it unto himself "for an everlasting sign that shall not be cut off." And, therefore, a wicked Bunyan, a degraded Newton, a contemptible thieving Moorhouse, a polluted and criminal McAuley, yes, and many a woman whose name is written upon His hands, if not the tablets of Christian fame, has been, in like manner made an especial monument of this cardinal principle of divine redemption, "where sin abounded grace did much more abound."

Oh, is there a soul reading these lines that conscience and the tempter have conspired to discourage on account of aggravated sin? It matters not how great the sin, how strange the aggravations, and how long the story of impenitence and even of unbelief. To you is this message spoken and you may echo back to the throne of grace the deep petition which inspiration long ago breathed from the lips of David, "For thine own sake, O Lord, pardon mine iniquity, for it is great."

But we, the people of God, must also fully realize this principle if we would stand prepared to fulfill the purpose of our Master. In this age the messengers have given forth the final invitations to the gospel feast. No longer are they to be chiefly addressed to the first invited guests, but it is from the highways and from the hedges and from the streets and lanes of the city that they are coming in today in great multitudes, and not only coming, but becoming the brightest trophies of redeeming grace and the most useful and honored instruments in the salvation of others. Shall we, beloved, fully realize the significance of this truth that the more lost, degraded and hopeless the soul may be to which we bring this precious gospel, the more willing is our Master to welcome it and the more glorious may be the issues of the redeemed life. As our faith in man decreases, thank God our faith in God rises to sublimer heights, that "where sin abounded grace shall much more abound."

II. This text is illustrated in the sanctification of believers and especially in their sanctification from qualities and tendencies naturally the most unholy and contrary to their new and sanctified lives. Still it is literally true in the deeper life of the soul that "where sin abounded grace much more abounds." It is not that God will make the good better, but that He will make the bad good, and the utterly and hopelessly bad divinely pure and holy. Sanctification is not the refining and elevating of the naturally pure, but the transforming of darkness into light, a selfish soul into a living sacrifice of love, and a heart all steeped in corruption into the glorious counterpart of Christ's own holiness. In the work of grace, God takes peculiar delight in contradicting natural probabilities and tendencies. He took a shrinking Jeremiah to be a bold and courageous reprover of Israel's prophets, priests and kings. He took a cowardly Peter to be the courageous and defiant apostle of Pentecost. He took a Son of Thunder to be the gentle, loving disciple of love. He took a raging persecutor to be the long-suffering apostle who could say, "I beseech you by the meekness and gentleness of Christ." He can make the weakest things in you the strongest, the worst things in you the occasions for the grace which will magnify in you the best and divinest qualities of the Christian life.

Beloved, shall we therefore cease to think and speak of the Christian life as a mere matter of education and fully realize that it is all a new creation and a miracle of infinite and omnipotent grace. All that God requires in each of us is an opportunity to show what He can do, and to prove over and over again that "where sin abounded grace shall much more abound."

III. The text is illustrated in the fact that divine grace not only saves and sanctifies but counteracts the consequences of his sins and more than triumphs over the sad and hurtful effects of the sin. Many a poor fellow thinks, and many a sermon we fear has helped him to think, that though he has been forgiven and saved, yet he need never expect to be delivered from the fruits of his life in harvests of sorrow and shame. He must not expect the consequences to be obviated but cheerfully endure them in patience and humility, thanking God that he has been saved from so much, and counting this but a reasonable reminder of the past and a very small retribution compared with what he deserved. He quotes, or others quote to him, a passage in Galations 6:7. "Whatsoever a man soweth that shall he also reap," and so they expect to reap in their bodies the physical infirmities and diseases which are the legitimate fruit of a life of dissipation and sin. They expect that their social and secular life may be embarrassed and impeded by the issues of their past, and that only after a long and patient endurance can they expect to recover themselves from the entanglement of the sins of their youth which encompassed them about.

Now we believe that grace is able to do something better than this, and that our blessed Lord has borne the bitter fruit of sin as our Substitute, and that His atonement has power to cancel all the effects of sin and even turn the curse into a blessing. The great Augustine, one of the fathers of the Christian Church, found himself at his conversion a physical wreck in his early youth. Every drop of his blood was poisoned by the virus of sin, and his frame was literally dropping into corruption through every abominable excess. But the grace of God not only saved his soul, but restored his body and gave him nearly half a century of almost unparalleled usefulness in physical health and strength and glorious service for his Master and the church.

Many a redeemed drunkard today can tell the same story of physical forces perfectly restored and every trace of a degraded life removed, not only from the physical energies but even from the very countenance. And so the grace of Christ can take the social life and counteract the innumerable currents of evil that have gone forth from us to return in our own life in entanglements and embarrassments and to work their lasting influences in the lives of others. In proportion to our faith, God can undo these influences and give us back all that we have lost and more. "I will restore to you," He says, "the years that the locust hath eaten, the cankerworm and the caterpiller, my great army which I sent among you." Sometimes the very life that the sinner has lived in the service of Satan is made an opportunity for greater usefulness, as he is enabled to reach classes to which the moral and respectable cannot even have access. And so God is constantly taking men out of the dives and slums, out of the saloons and dance-halls, out of the great lost world, that He may send them back again to their own former sphere as messengers of redeeming love. Fear not, then, poor trembling disciple, that you shall be drawn into the vortex that your own past life has created. Reckon yourself dead indeed unto it in all its issues, and go forth claiming the full redemption of your risen Lord and walking with Him as though you were not even the same person who once lived the life of sin and misery.

IV. The text is illustrated most sublimely of all in the work of redemption. In a word its deep significance is simply this, that the work of Christ's redemption has more than counteracted and will ultimately transcend all the effects of the Fall. We believe that it has brought more glory to God than if the human race had kept its first estate. It has led to a new revelation of the divine characer, which, but for sin might never have been known. Creation revealed God in His power, wisdom and purity, but only redemption has revealed Him in His attitude of grace, that is, divine goodness dealing with the sinful and the lost. Had man never fallen, God would certainly have been known as a holy Being, through the terrible retribution which He visited upon the angels which kept not their first estate; but the wreck of the human race has exhibited Him in the most beautiful and attractive of all attitudes as the God of mercy and love to the unworthy and wicked. Heaven would often have heard the song, "Alleluia! for the Lord God Omnipotent reigneth," even if Christ never had died, but only redemption has given the key-note of the new song, "Worthy is the Lamb that was slain!"

But it is not only an exhibition of His love and grace, but of that transcendent wisdom that could still vindicate His righteousness and guard the sanctity of His holy will, and yet devise a way by which mercy could have free exercise and God could be just and yet a Saviour. The cross of Jesus Christ becomes a monument of God's infinite wisdom, righteousness and love, and through all the ages to come will exhibit "the exceeding riches of his grace in his kindness towards us by Jesus Christ." Take out of the coming eternity the song of redemption, the millennial kingdom, the glory of Jesus and the prospects of His redeemed people, and heaven would seem annihilated and the universe a dreary waste, while even God Himself would become enveloped in clouds of thickest, darkest and remotest distance, and the Bible would be obliterated from existence.

The benefits that come to men are still more manifest and deeply interesting. The redemption of our fallen race brings us to a far higher place than the first creation ever gave us. Unfallen man was only a creature made in the image of God, but a little lower than the angels. Redeemed man has been raised above the rank of angels to partake of the very nature of God, to be a joint-heir with the Son of God and to share eternally the throne of his Creator and the attributes of the eternal Son, our glorious Head. Redemption is therefore not the restoration of

Adamic holiness, happiness or honor, but it is the uniting of man with the Son of God and the exalting of the redeemed sinner to kindred fellowship with a higher Being, so that, eternally like his Lord, the redeemed man shall be, not only a man, but a man united with God and possessing in the depths of his being the very spirit and nature of the eternal Jehovah.

This is so sublime that we would fear to boldly state it, had we not the unmistakable language of the Holy Scriptures. "Behold what manner of love the Father hath bestowed upon us that we should be called the sons of God." "Beloved, now are we the sons of God, and it doth not yet appear what we shall be: but we know that when he shall appear, we shall be like him; for we shall see him as he is." "Whereby are given unto us exceeding great and precious promises: that by these ye might be partakers of the divine nature." ". . . your life is hid with Christ in God. When Christ, who is our life, shall appear, then shall ye also appear with him in glory." Yes, the day is coming when Satan shall gaze upon the consummated work of the Great Restorer and see everything his hand has touched transformed into a monument of the grace and power of the Redeemer, and even he shall bow the knee and bitterly confess like one of his ancient disciples, "Oh, Nazarene! Thou hast conquered."

We may not be able to understand all sides of this great problem. Of course it would not be right to say that God intended or desired the sin and fall of His creatures and the sad train of still greater sin and misery that has followed. But we can surely believe that while He discountenanced the disobedience of Adam, as He does all disobedience, while He desires His children to walk in His will in holy obedience, and while He still is deeply grieved with every transgression and something is lost by it inevitably, yet the resources of His grace and power are such that, being committed, He has ample expedients to counteract its effects; and while all the consequences are not averted, yet enough good is brought out of it to result, in the end, in a higher aggregate of blessing, to turn the evil to the best possible account, and to show that God's all-sufficiency is more than a match for every emergency that can ever arise.

For ourselves, surely, the practical lessons are not hard to find. If there be a discouraged life within reach of this message, if there is a heart that has been held back by the iron fetters of the past and to whom Satan has been whispering, "There is no hope, but we will go on in the imagination of our hearts," oh, beloved, surely we have seen enough in this passage to answer the unworthy thought and ignoble fear, and to encourage us just because of the extremity of our situation, to claim more boldly, the interposition of our Almighty Friend and the over-ruling power of His grace and love. The very hardest case is the one which He most loves to take. The most hopeless situation is the one through whose relief He is most glorified. If everything in your life seems against you, and if, worst of all, you feel that you alone are to blame for everything that is against you; if it has been, not only sorrow but sin, and every aggravation of sin—beloved, the grace of Jesus Christ was prepared for you and such as you. Only prove its all-sufficiency and you shall be among all that we have already specified, the crowning illustration of this most blessed truth, that "where sin abounded grace did much more abound."

God's great ultimate purpose for His redeemed people is the key to all the "exceeding great and precious promises." This, and this alone, explains the strong language in which He speaks to us of the provisions of His grace for our needs. These promises are out of all proportion to our importance or worth, and it is not strange that naturally we should hesitate to accept such boundless and stupendous assurances of love and care, and that our faith should be as narrow and paltry as it often is. It is not strange that the beggar child should be content with rags and crumbs, and almost think it is mocked when you talk to it about palaces and offer it the costly robes and the princely treasures of royalty. The truth is, we are the children naturally of low and shameful birth and spiritual destitution, but we have been adopted into a higher rank, nay, we have been born into a heavenly life and a divine sonship, and we are destined, as the very children of God, to share the exceeding riches of His glory through all the ages to come; and, therefore, we are recognized by Him now and treated in the manner befitting our future glory. We are like the children of wealthy parents who are at school in a foreign land, not having yet come into their inheritance, but being supplied by their father, even in their minority, with boundless wealth for every need. And so, although we have not entered upon our eternal inheritance, yet God has given us a cheque book on the bank of heaven, and on the back of every cheque He has Himself endorsed the vast and illimitable guarantee, "My God shall supply all your need according to his riches in glory by Jesus Christ."

And so this word "abound" has come to be a sort of a key-note to the New Testament promises. Even of His promises He says, "Wherein God, willing more abundantly to shew unto the heirs of promise the immutability of his counsel, confirmed it by an oath" (Heb. 6:17). His word is abundant, His promises boundless, His loving, faithful heart struggles to express in ever ampler language and larger utterance, the immeasurable and unspeakable fullness of His love, so that His great promises are like mountains piled upon mountains until His faithfulness truly reacheth unto the clouds.

So again, His mercy and grace to the sinful are as abundant. "The grace of our Lord," says the Apostle, "was exceeding abundant with faith and love which is in Christ Jesus." And again in Romans 5:17, he speaks of those who ". . . receive abundance of grace and the gift of righteousness shall reign in life by one, Jesus Christ." The life that Jesus brings to us is not only life but "life more abundantly" (John 10:10). Redemption and forgiveness are declared in Ephesians 1:7, 8, to be ". . . according to the riches of his grace; wherein he hath abounded toward us in all wisdom and prudence," that is, in all the variety of the love and care that adapts and adjusts His mercy and His grace to every shade of guilt and need, and which anticipates every future emergency; for this is the meaning of "prudence," literally, foresight and providence.

His purpose in our salvation is that "in the ages to come he might shew the exceeding riches of his grace in his kindness toward us through Christ Jesus" (Eph. 2:7). All the dispensations of His providence are destined to give occasion for still larger manifestations of His grace, "For all things are for your sakes, that the abundant grace might through the thanksgiving of many redound to the glory of God" (2 Cor. 4:15). Even in our deepest sorrows He has made provision for such overflowing abundance of comfort and joy that the sorrow shall be lost in the joy, for, "As the sufferings of Christ abound in us, so our consolation also aboundeth by Christ" (2 Cor. 1:5). The provisions of grace for our Christian life and work are equally boundless, for "God is able to make all grace abound toward you; that ye, always having all sufficiency in all things, may abound to every good work" (2 Cor. 9:8). And like a mountain-top, high above all the rest and lost in the clouds, it is all summed up in the sublime hyperbole, "Now unto him that is able to do exceeding abundantly above all that we ask or think, according to the power that worketh in us, unto him be glory in the church by Christ Jesus throughout all ages, world without end. Amen" (Eph. 3:20, 21).

This is the divine measure of redeeming grace, and so on our side we are called upon to meet God's high measure with corresponding fullness. We are to abound in faith. "Rooted and built up in him, and stablished in the faith, as ye have been taught, abounding therein with thanksgiving" (Col. 2:7). We are to abound in love. "And this I pray, that your love may abound yet more and more in knowledge and in all judgment" (Phil. 1:9). "And the Lord make you to increase and abound in love one toward another, and toward all men, even as we do toward you" (1 Thes. 3:12). We are to abound in holiness. "Furthermore then we beseech you, brethren, and exhort you by the Lord Jesus, that as ye have received of us how ye ought to walk and to please God, so ye would abound more and more" (1 Thes. 4:1). We are to abound in joy. "That your rejoicing may be more abundant in Jesus Christ" (Phil. 1:26), and in hope, "Now the God of hope fill you with all joy and peace in believing, that ye may abound in hope, through the power of the Holy Ghost" (Rom. 15:13). We are to abound in liberality, even in the depths of poverty. "The abundance of their joy and their deep poverty abounded unto the riches of their liberality." "Therefore as ye abound in everything, in faith, and utterance, and knowledge, and in all diligence, and in your love to us, see that ye abound in this grace also" (2 Cor. 8:2, 7).

And our spiritual experience is to be not a strained but an ample one, ever growing in breadth, depth, height and symmetry, through the abundant grace of the divine nature in our heart. "And beside this, giving all diligence, add to your faith virtue; and to virtue knowledge; and to knowledge temperance; and to temperance patience; and to patience godliness; and to godliness brotherly kindness; and to brotherly kindness charity. For if these things be in you, and abound, they make you that ye shall neither be barren nor unfruitful in the knowledge of our Lord Jesus Christ" (2 Pet. 1:5-8). And finally if we thus enter into His abundant grace we shall have His glorious recompense in like proportion, and "So an entrance shall be ministered unto you abundantly into the everlasting kingdom of our Lord and Saviour Jesus Christ."

Beloved, shall we so receive "His fullness, even grace for grace," and so enter in at last, not like a battered ship, with masts and sails all gone and banner torn to shreds, and slowly drawn by some old tug boat across the bar into the harbor or the drydock; but shall we rather, with flags all flying, and sails swelling in the gales of heaven, and myriads on the shore waiting to welcome us, shall we have an entrance ministered unto us abundantly into the everlasting kingdom of our Lord and Saviour Jesus Christ, while wondering angels, looking back to the past and gazing in amazement on our present glory, shall turn to each other and say, "where sin abounded grace did much more abound."

VIII From Strength to Strength

"From strength to strength"
[Psalm 84:7].

THIS is a chapter of the "Pilgrim's Progress" through the valley of Baca, of which this beautiful psalm is a picture. It is the story of the life of trust, and its two keynotes are the fifth and twelfth verses of the psalm, "O Lord of hosts, blessed is the man that trusteth in thee." "Blessed is the man whose strength is in thee." To him the valley of Baca, the valley of weeping, at once becomes a well of living waters, and every low and dry place a pool for the heavenly rain to fill with floods of deeper blessing; and drinking from the living waters the pilgrims go "from strength to strength," and all at last go home, for "every one of them in Zion appeareth before God."

"From strength to strength!" But there is a previous chapter, from weakness to strength. For man is naturally the weakest creature in the universe. He comes into life with the wail of a helpless infant, weaker than the tiger's cub or the birdling in its nest. But his physical frailty is but a figure of his spiritual helplessness. "When we were yet without strength, in due time Christ died for the ungodly." But the grace of God in the conversion of the soul brings its first spiritual strength, enabling it to choose and trust the Lord, to turn from sin and walk in holy obedience. Then it sings the new song, "O Lord, I will praise thee: though thou wast angry with me, thine anger is turned away, and thou comfortedst me. Behold, God is my salvation; I will trust, and be not afraid: for the Lord Jehovah is my strength and my song; he also is become my salvation."

Very strong is the new-born trust and love of the converted soul; very strong its purpose, its joy and its holy enthusiasm. It truly seems as if it never could be tempted to doubt or disobey, and, like Peter, it is ready to cry, "Though all men should deny thee, yet will I never deny thee." And God meets us on this plane and helps our strength, although He has something far better for us further on. Speaking to such a heart in the forty-first of Isaiah and the ninth verse, He says, "Thou art my servant; I have chosen thee, and not cast thee away." It is the experience of the soul that has just come to God. And then He adds, "Fear thou not; for I am with thee: be not dismayed; for I am thy God: I will strengthen thee; yea, I will help thee; yea, I will uphold thee with the right hand of my righteousness."

These last three clauses describe three very distinct experiences of our early Christian life. The first comes when we begin to feel our strength insufficient and cry to God for increased strength, and He strengthens us. It is the old kind of strength, but He gives us more of it. But soon even this is not sufficient, and, as we still sink, He comes and adds His help to our strength. "I will help thee," He says. It is now the strengthened heart with the strong Lord helping. But still you will notice that we are in front and not the Lord. It is our battle, and He is simply reinforcing us with His auxiliaries. But now a greater crisis comes. Even this is not sufficient, and we sink in the conflict and are ready to fall in utter exhaustion and discouragement, when lo! our Mighty Helper comes upon the field Himself, takes the battle in His own almighty hands, lifts up our sinking form as a mother would a babe, bids us no longer to stand even in His help, but takes us bodily in His arms and carries us with His own almighty strength as He cries, "Yea, I will uphold thee with the right hand of my righteousness."

Oh, that is from strength to strength! From our own strength to His increased strength, and now from even this to the absolute all-sufficiency of God Himself.

Now we notice in the vivid imagery of the prophet a sudden and complete change upon the battlefield, and looking round, we find that all our foes have already fled before His face. Our almighty Captain has taken the field, and "lo! all they that were incensed against thee shall be ashamed and confounded, and they that strive with thee shall perish. Thou shalt seek them and not find them, even them that contended with thee; they that war against thee shall be as nothing, and as a thing of nought."

In the third chapter of Revelation we see the little church of Philadelphia going through something like this experience. "Thou hast a little strength," the Master says, "and hast kept my word and not denied my name." But in the tenth verse we find a mightier strength coming to the faithful in Philadelphia. "Because thou hast kept the word of my patience I also will keep thee." It is God's keeping now, not our own; and in the twelfth verse it reached its climax. The one who had "a little strength" has now become "a pillar," with strength enough not only to uphold its own weight, but to support the edifice under which it stands. But when Philadelphia becomes a pillar its own individuality passes away, and it becomes identified with God Himself, for He says, "I will write upon him the name of my God, and the name of the city of my God, which is New Jerusalem, which cometh down out of heaven from my God; and I will write upon him my new name." This is not now mere human strength, but the strength of Jehovah.

We have now got to the great theme which we desire to impress as the Lord enables us.

I. It is divine, not human strength, and it is strength

which is wholly divine and in no sense or measure human. It is an exchange of strength in which we have surrendered all our fancied power and received instead the divine power and enabling. This glorious exchange of strength is vividly set forth in the animated language of the sublime Isaiah, chapter 40: "He giveth power to the faint, and to them that have no might he increaseth strength. Even the youths shall faint and be weary, and the young men shall utterly fall, but they that wait upon the Lord shall exchange their strength." That is to say, the strongest human strength, the manhood of young men, the vigor and vitality of youth shall be wholly inadequate for the exigencies of Christian life and conflict, and it is not until these have failed that God has room to display the resources of His omnipotence. When we become "faint," then He giveth His power, and when we have "no might," then He "increaseth strength," and that is, gives yet more because of our utter helplessness. Waiting on the Lord, we let our strength go and take His instead, and so renew or exchange our strength.

A simple figure may help to illustrate the thought. Look at that man trying to ford a river, and with all his might struggling with the deep flood, and, by dint of tremendous physical exertions, stemming its mighty waters, and panting and exhausted reaching the other shore. That is strength matched with the strength of the elements. But look at another. Wading out a little distance into the deep flood by the exercise of his own strength, he now lets go, and falls and sinks upon the bosom of the river. Lo! it bears him without a struggle and carries him down in its swift current. He has let go his strength, and he is now carried by the strength of the stream.

So there are many of us who are trying to ford the stream by our own strong will and efforts. There is a sweeter way, by ceasing from our strength and falling into the mighty current of God's infinite life and love and being borne by a power superior to ours without a struggle. Many people never reach their true development until their difficulties become so great that they break down in the struggle and fall into the arms of God. This is what the apostle meant when he exclaimed, "I take pleasure in infirmities; when I am weak then am I strong." And this was but an echo of the Master's own assurance, "My grace is sufficient for thee, for my strength is made perfect in weakness."

Beloved, have you exchanged your strength for the Lord's? Have you gone "from strength," that is yours, "to strength," that is the strength divine!

II. It is strength for a higher spiritual plane. "They shall mount up with wings as eagles." It is a strength which enables us to mount to a higher element of life and communion with God. It brings us into the divine life and raises us up to dwell in heavenly places with Christ. It resists and overcomes the natural direction of earth, to draw us downward, and, like the buoyant wing of the fowls of the firmament, it bears us and holds us on high, in a calm and heavenly atmosphere where the world lies beneath our feet, and we are lifted above the things which once encompassed and entangled us. We are not now fighting the wild waves, but flying far above them in another element. The mightiest human strength cannot lift us up to this. Only the strong pinions of the Heavenly Dove can bear us aloft to, and hold us supremely in this heavenly region. This is God's true deliverance from most of our troubles; not to change them, but to rise above them. Oh, how we need these seasons of spiritual elevation and heavenly inspiration to strengthen us for the practical sphere of common life, and enable us to "run and not be weary"; and to "walk and not faint."

Yes we need these times of waiting,
  When their strength our souls renew:
Drinking at the heavenly fountain,
  Bathing in the heavenly dew;
Yes, we need these heights of rapture,
  When we mount on eagles' wings,
Then returning to earth's duties,
  All our heart exultant springs.
Oh how every labor lightens!
  As with swift divine constraint,
We can "run and not be weary,"
  We can "walk and never faint."

III. Strength for the practical duties of life. For they that thus "renew their strength" "shall run and not be weary"; and "they shall walk and not faint." It is not all for heights of rapture or hours of vision, but these experiences reach their true fruition in the consecration of our common life and the triumph of faith and patience in the routine of daily duty. This is the pathway where we have often to run the strong race of peculiar difficulty, strenuous exertion and sudden and severe emergency, but God's strength does not grow weary under the most extreme tests. Then there are the long protracted strains, the almost interminable delays, the endless minutiæ of trial, irritation and care, that need the sustained strength which holds on its way and carries us through all the details of life's experiences as victoriously as through its greater battlefields. These are the things that exhaust mere human strength, but the strength of God can "walk and not faint." Beloved, have we thus exchanged our strength and are we victoriously pursuing our onward way with calm, victorious spirit, unwearied and unfainting?

IV. It is strength to "withstand in the evil day and having done all to stand." Dr. Mackay of Hull once said that Isaiah had left out one of the things which God's strength enables us to do, for it is harder to run than to fly, and harder to walk than to run, but there is something harder than walking, and that is to stand. Now Paul has supplied this omission, if it be one, in his superb picture of the Christian conqueror in the sixth chapter of Ephesians. This chapter, by the way, is the very chapter of the life that has mounted up with wings as eagles and is dwelling on high. Its keynote is, "Dwelling in heavenly places in Christ Jesus," and, like the picture in Isaiah, the apostle ends with a very practical conclusion. The outcome of all this strength is to "put on the whole armor of God, that ye may be able to stand against the wiles of the devil. For we wrestle not against flesh and blood, but against principalities, against powers, against the rulers of the darkness of this world, against spiritual wickedness in high places. Wherefore take unto you the whole armor of God, that ye may be able to withstand in the evil day, and having done all, to stand." This is the only strength which will enable you to stand. The sooner we discover the better, that the strongest of us is no match for Satan, and that our highest and holiest resolutions will be surely broken and our souls trodden down in defeat and despair beneath our conqueror's scornful feet, unless we meet our spiritual foes in the very presence and power of Jesus.

For this is just what all this picture means. The shield of faith is the faith of God; the sword of the Spirit is the Word of God, wielded by the Holy Ghost within us; the very prayer in which we are to overcome is to be prayed in the Spirit; the armor is the armor of God; the strength is to "be strong in the Lord and the power of his might." In a word, it is to confront the devil with the living God within us and so possessing us that the battle is not ours but God's, and the enemy, from the beginning, understands that he has challenged, not a poor unequal man, but his own Almighty Conqueror, the Son of God.

This is to be "more than conqueror through him that loved us"; this is to say, "Thanks be unto God, who always causeth us to triumph in Christ."

V. It is strength to endure. Let us read attentively Colossians 1:11. "Strengthened with all might, according to his glorious power, unto all patience and longsuffering with joyfulness." Here is one of the advanced stations of the pilgrim's progress "from strength to strength." We may well pause and ask if we have reached this place of strength. Is this then the goal of Pentecost? Is this the great objective point contemplated by the mighty baptism of the Holy Ghost? Is this the meaning of the power from on high? "Strengthened with all might according to his glorious power!" One would surely look for a sublimer battlefield to follow such a splendid parade of the armies of God. But lo! We behold an entirely different spectacle. A solitary soldier on an obscure and weary pathway, battling with a thousand petty hardships, difficulties and trials, or standing through all the day of battle without a single opportunity of advancing, and seemingly called to nothing else but to stand under the fire of the enemy and to "endure hardness as a good soldier of Jesus Christ." His whole business seems to be "patience and longsuffering"; the first, with reference to the trials which God is pleased to send upon him; the second, the annoyances and injuries of men. Ah! these are the very things human strength cannot endure. Many a brave man can stand under a cannon's fire more calmly than he can endure the taunts of a fellow-creature. The highest victory of the Son of God was, that, "when he was reviled he reviled not again; when he suffered he threatened not": and the mightiest triumphs of the strength of God in us are realized when we can receive the hiding of our Father's face and even the weight of His mighty hand without a doubt or murmur, and accept the misconceptions, opprobriums, reproaches and wrongs of our fellowmen, not only with longsuffering, but with joyfulness; not only unruffled and unretaliating, but sweetly realizing and fully believing that they are to us the pledges of some richer blessing from our heavenly Father, and the guarantees of something so glorious that we cannot but thank God for giving us the opportunity of thus winning another blessing.

Beloved, have we any room for progress here "from strength to strength"?

VI. It is strength that carries us in victory through the whole range of our Christian experience with all its extremes, and enables us to say, "I can do all things through Christ which strengtheneth me." The apostle had tested it in the heights and depths of human circumstances and found it equal to all vicissitudes, variations and exigencies. The force of his glorious confession lies in the "all things." Human strength can accomplish some things, but the strength of God is equally adequate for all. It is equal in its uniformity, immutability, unvariableness. Over every opening morning it inscribes the promise, "As thy day so shall thy strength be." It has such an infinite reserve of all-sufficiency that we need not question whether our strength is adequate to the duty. All we need to know is, does God require it? for if He does He will abundantly enable us. The great ships of ocean, and especially the ships of today, are scarcely affected by the storms or the elements. They are so strong that they move on with equal facility through the glassy sea or the rolling waves. The strength of God in a human life will carry it thus steadily through all life's changes.

"Calm as the ray of sun or star,
Which storms assail in vain,
Moving unruffled through life's war,
The eternal calm to gain."

VII. It is strength which enables us to receive Christ's indwelling in all its fullness, and to enter into all the meaning of His mystical life. "For this cause I bow my knees unto the Father of our Lord Jesus Christ, of whom the whole family in heaven and earth is named, that he would grant you, according to the riches of his glory, to be strengthened with might by his Spirit in the inner man; that Christ may dwell in your hearts by faith; that ye, being rooted and grounded in love, may be able to comprehend with all saints what is the breadth, and length, and depth, and height; and to know the love of Christ, which passeth knowledge, that ye might be filled with all the fulness of God. Now unto him that is able to do exceeding abundantly above all that we ask or think, according to the power that worketh in us, unto him be glory in the church by Christ Jesus throughout all ages, world without end. Amen."

The apostle is speaking here of the indwelling of God in the heart; "That ye might be filled with all the fulness of God," is the crowning statement of this great truth and experience. This is possible in a measure "exceeding abundantly above" all that we are enabled to ask or think. It is to be realized through Christ dwelling in our hearts, and Christ's indwelling will bring us into an experience of love in which we shall know and comprehend the height and depth and length and breadth of His love which passeth all knowledge. But this indwelling of Christ comes through simple faith. Now all this looks extremely easy on paper and in theory, but the apostle tells us that in order to enter into it we must be "strengthened with might by his Spirit in the inner man." This divine filling requires a vessel that can hold it, and a vessel supernaturally strengthened. You cannot put a charge of dynamite or a hundred-pound shot into a pocket pistol or a vessel of clay. You want the mightiest ordnance, the strongest barrel and breech, to bear the enormous strain of so much concentrated power. And God has to prepare us as the vessels of His power, and, in order to do so, He must take us out of our own strength into the strength of Christ. Our mere natural capacities cannot receive Jesus. The loftiest intellect, the strongest brain, is unequal to this experience; but the humblest capacity, when strengthened by the Holy Ghost, may know God as no angel ever knew Him, and exult in His immeasurable love, as only His loved ones can.

And even after we have received Christ's indwelling through the Holy Ghost enabling us, there are depths and heights in "all the fullness of God" in which we more perfectly enter, in proportion as we allow the Holy Ghost to fit us for the deeper and higher experience. This is often what our severest trials are meant for, to give to our spirit a vigor and capacity which will enable us to rise to a higher place in the fellowship.

VIII. It is strength which is established and perfected by spiritual discipline. "But the God of all grace, who hath called us unto his eternal glory by Christ Jesus, after that ye have suffered a while, make you perfect, stablish, strengthen, settle you" (1 Pet. 5:10). Every new experience of Christ's grace must be confirmed by some new discipline in the school of trial, and even after we have come to know God as "the God of all grace, who hath called us unto his eternal glory," we must suffer a while, that even this knowledge and experience of His grace may be established, strengthened, settled.

And so we are ever passing on "from strength to strength," and finding, like the giant oak, that the wildest tempests, instead of tearing us from our foundation, only plant us deeper and root us the more securely to the Rock of Ages.

IX

God's Measureless Measures

"But they measuring themselves by themselves, and comparing themselves among themselves are not wise. But we will not boast of things without our measure, but according to the measure of the rule which God hath distributed to us, a measure to reach even unto you" [2 Cor. 10:12, 13].

"With what measure ye mete, it shall be measured to you: and unto you that hear shall more be given" [Mark 4:24].

WE HAVE here two sorts of measures contrasted, the human and the divine. There is a great deal in a measure. Half an inch off the draper's yardstick makes a good many yards difference when the goods are delivered. The division of a hair line in a carpenter's rule might destroy all the calculations of the architect in the construction of a building. A little boy told his mother that he was six feet high, and when she doubted the statement he assured her that he had just measured himself by his own little rule. His calculations would have been all right if his rule had been right, but when examined, it was found to be a little less than six inches long. This is the sort of rule that a great many Christians measure by.

There are two sorts of human measures; the one is when we are "measuring ourselves by ourselves"; the other, when we are "comparing ourselves among ourselves"; that is, measuring by others. Both are equally "unwise," for both come equally short of the divine rule. Many persons are always trying to measure up to their ideal and their aspirations and to the out-reaching of their poor souls, and the lofty ideals of humanity, as they are pleased to call them. They will tell us that they have lived up to their light and to their conscience and are satisfied with their opinions and content with their lives, and that it is nobody's business but their own. They are measuring themselves by themselves. Some who have come upon a higher plane are measuring themselves by a past experience, by some memory of blessing, some little Mizar or some lofty mount to which they have risen in the distant past, and this, to them, is the type and ideal of all their life. And so, we find thousands trying to hold on to their experience or to get it back again, instead of remembering that God is "able to do exceeding abundantly above all that we ask or think."

Others again are ever comparing themselves with others, congratulating themselves that they are as good as some of their standard, or aiming to resemble some human ideal. The result of this is to be seen in the human traditions and the stereotyped patterns of Christian living, according to which so many are moulding their dwarfed and wretched lives. All this is but human measuring; all this is most unwise. From all this Paul turned to reach up to God's measure, and, forgetting the things which were behind, he pressed toward the mark for the prize of the high calling of God in Christ Jesus, striving that he might apprehend that for which he was apprehended of Christ Jesus. It is a great thing to have a worthy ideal or pattern. It is better to aim high and miss it than it is to aim low and reach it. The famous artist was wise when he wept with bitter tears because he had reached his ideal. He could dream of nothing higher than he had achieved with his brush and to him the charm and inspiration of life had gone.

We find a number of God's standards and measures referred to in the Holy Scriptures, rising like the rounds of Jacob's ladder from earth to heaven. There is a simple phrase often repeated in the New Testament and often overlooked, which expresses these measures and steppings. It is the phrase "according to," two words which rise like the uprights of Jacob's ladder to the heavens, and across which many of the precious promises may be seen in the vision of faith firmly fastened as heavenly steps leading higher and higher up to all the good and perfect will of God. Let us glance at some of these heavenly measures.

I. The Will of God

This is at once the limitation and the inspiration of our faith and prayer. "If we ask anything according to his will, he heareth us." "The Spirit maketh intercession for the saints according to the will of God." Beyond this our desires and our aspirations cannot go, but beyond it they need not desire to go, for within it lie all the probabilities of blessing which a human and immortal life can receive; and God's chief desire is to get us to see how much it means of blessing for us. As we have often said, there is no vaster prayer within the reach of faith than the simple sentence, "Thy will be done." This will must mean for each of us our highest possible good. We know it includes our salvation, if we will accept salvation, for "God will have all men to be saved." We know it includes our sanctification, for "this is the will of God, even your sanctification." We know it includes our deliverance from physical evil if we will receive it in His Name in faith and obedience, for He has said, "I will. Be thou clean." We know it includes every needed blessing that the obedient can require, for He has said, "he will withhold no good thing from them that walk uprightly." The apostle's prayer for his beloved friends was that they might have fulfilled in them "all the good pleasure of his goodness"; and that they might "prove that good and acceptable and perfect will of God."

Beloved, are you measuring up to this divine rule? Are you meeting all your Father's will? Are you walking "worthy of him to all pleasing," and having fulfilled the benediction and prayer, that He may "make you perfect in every good work to do his will, working in you that which is wellpleasing in his sight, through Jesus Christ; to whom be glory forever and ever. Amen."

II. His Word

"Behold, the handmaid of the Lord!" is the sublime response of Mary to the angel's astonishing message, "be it unto me according to thy word." Never was faith put to harder test. Never was woman asked to stand in so delicate a place of peril and possibility, of humbling shame, and glorious everlasting honor. Realizing perhaps with every instinct of her maiden heart all that this might cost her, she meekly, unhesitatingly, without one question, one faltering breath, accepted the stupendous promise and responsibility, and rose to meet the divine measure, "according to thy word," and like an echo came back the heavenly benediction, "Blessed is she that believed: for there shall be a performance of those things that were told her from the Lord."

Beloved, are you living up to this great measure? Is faith resting and claiming, not according to signs and seemings, frames and feelings, but according to His word? Is obedience walking, not according to the course of this world, or the moods of our capricious hearts, or the standards of men, or the example of others, or the traditions even of the church, but according to His word? Are we Bible Christians and determined to believe and obey every word within these inspired and heavenly pages? Then we shall be found in "the way everlasting," for "the grass withereth and the flower fadeth, but the Word of our God shall stand forever," and "he that doeth the will of God abideth forever."

III. The Riches of His Grace

"In whom we have redemption through his blood, the forgiveness of sins, according to the riches of his grace;

wherein he hath abounded toward us in all wisdom and prudence." Peter has used a parallel expression. "According to his abundant mercy hath begotten us again unto a lively hope." This is God's standard and measure of salvation. He works and saves according to the riches of His grace. He abounds towards us in all wisdom and prudence, that is, He adapts His mercy to every variety of guilt, and He anticipates, in His prudence and foresight every future emergency. He sees Peter from the beginning to the end of his career and accepts him "for better or for worse"; and when the hour of his shameful fall is near, He can say, "I have prayed for thee." So He takes every one of us and adjusts His infinite grace to all the minutiæ of our sin and its worst aggravations, our corrupt and ruined nature and all its wreck, our weak and helpless will and all its inability to stand, our circumstances, our temptations and all that besets us. Knowing and anticipating all, He just encompasses us in His everlasting arms and saves and keeps us, "according to the riches of his grace."

Beloved, have you entered into the fullness of this measure and have you understood it in all its all-sufficiency for a lost world and the most wretched and ruined lives over whom you pray and love? Oh, let our faith look up from lost humanity, to the mighty love of God and "the exceeding riches of his grace." And if there be a discouraged and guilty soul within reach of this message, may God help you, beloved one, to put your sins with all their aggravations side by side with God's immeasurable grace, until you shall realize something of the Psalmist's sublime figure when he sang, "For as the heaven is high above the earth, so great is his mercy toward them that fear him. As far as the east is from the west, so far hath he removed our transgressions from us." Our sins may have reached to the clouds until they have become like a "thick cloud," but, thank God, "his mercy is in the heavens," and far above the clouds.

IV. THE RICHES OF HIS GLORY

Can we form any conception of the riches of His glory? Moses asked to see that glory but was told it was too bright for human gaze and only in the distance and from behind could he dare to look upon it. A little glimpse of it the disciples beheld on the Mount of Transfiguration, but they were afraid of its brightness and their eyes were overcome with slumber under its spell. "The heavens declare his glory and the firmament showeth his handiwork," and some conception of the riches of His power and majesty may be gathered from these glorious constellations and worlds of light which science is more fully exploring in these wondrous days. Sometimes we have sat down and allowed our minds to dwell on the multitude of these discoveries and calculations. We have tried to take in the magnitude of yonder planet many hundred times larger than our world, and yonder sun outweighing the world many thousandfold, and stars beyond stars,

> "Where system into systems runs
> And other planets circle other suns."

until our brain whirls and threatens to collapse under the pressure of the sublimity; and "lo! these are parts of his ways: but the thunder of his power who can understand?" His hand holds all these orbs; His will commands all these forces; His wisdom poises all these spheres and directs them in their course without a jar or catastrophe; His sceptre sways this mighty empire; His creating word called every portion of it into being; His providence upholds it every moment; His taste and goodness have adorned it with beauty and loveliness and enriched it with happiness and blessing. There is not a creature among its inhabitants from the highest archangel to the lowest insect but owes its being to His power and goodness. And all this is but "the hiding of his power" for His omnipotence could call millions of such universes into being in a moment. Nay, all this is but a scaffolding for the glory which He is preparing for the abode of His redeemed. The riches of His glory will not be complete until the new heavens and earth shall have emerged from the flames of a dissolving world and the New Jerusalem descended from heaven in the glory of God with streets of gold and gates of pearl and foundations of precious gems, and all the thrones are reared, and crowns are set, and the mansions are completed, and the glorified are shining "as the sun in the kingdom of their Father," and we ourselves are crowned with all "the riches of his glory."

Oh, beloved! we shall then understand something of the meaning of such verses as these, "I pray that God would grant you according to the riches of his glory, to be strengthened by his Spirit in the inner man, that Christ may dwell in your hearts by faith." Or again, "Strengthened with all might, according to his glorious power, unto all patience and longsuffering with joyfulness." Or again, "My God shall supply all your need according to his riches in glory by Christ Jesus." It is according to the riches of His glory that He is working out the new creation in our hearts and preparing the more glorious temple of the soul for His own eternal abode. It is according to the riches of His glory that He is willing to strengthen the heart for all patience and longsuffering. And it is according to the riches of His glory that He is able and ready to supply all our need. There is nothing too hard for such a God, too rich and glorious for His wisdom, grace and love. He looks at the littleness of our faith and cries, "Hast thou not known? hast thou not heard, that the everlasting God, the Lord, the Creator of the ends of the earth, fainteth not, neither is weary? there is no searching of his understanding. He giveth power to the faint; and to them that have no might he increaseth strength."

Beloved, let us lift up our eyes and behold the glory of our God and begin to walk as sons and heirs, and claim, even in our minority, something of the riches of His glory.

V. THE RESURRECTION AND ASCENSION OF JESUS CHRIST

"That ye may know what is the hope of his calling, and what the riches of the glory of his inheritance in the saints, and what is the exceeding greatness of his power to usward who believe, according to the working of his mighty power, which he wrought in Christ, when he raised him from the dead, and set him at his own right hand in the heavenly places, far above all principality, and power, and might, and dominion, and every name that is named, not only in this world, but also in that which is to come: and hath put all things under his feet, and gave him to be the head over all things to the church, which is his body, the fulness of him that filleth all in all."

The resurrection and ascension of Jesus Christ have become for us the pledge and pattern of all our faith and hope can claim. The power that God hath wrought in Christ in raising Him from the dead and setting Him upon His own right hand is the very same power which we may expect Him to exercise to usward who believe. "The riches of the glory of this inheritance in the saints" is the standard of what we may share in our spiritual experience now. God has performed for us the most stupendous miracle of grace and power and nothing can ever be too hard or too high for us to expect from "the God and Father of our Lord Jesus Christ." The picture is a very definite as well as a very glorious one. Step by step we can ascend its transcendent and celestial heights with our ascending Lord, as we see Him rise, first above the mighty power of death, and then above and "far above all principality and power and might and dominion and every name that is named, not only in this world but in that which is to come," until all things are beneath His feet. And then as we gaze upon His lofty preëminence we are permitted to sit down by His side and claim all the fullness of His glory as our own. For all His ascension power and majesty are, not for His own personal exaltation, but that He might become the Head over all things for His body the church, and He takes His high preëminence as our Representative and recognizes us as already seated with Him in the heavenly place. His resurrection therefore, involves ours, His triumphs ours, His ascension ours, His rights are shared with us.

Do we require in our behalf the exercise of an authority that transcends all other authority? We have but to remember that He, our exalted Head, is sitting far above all principalities. Do we require a force to be exercised for us over-matching the mightiest forces of nature or of evil? He is sitting far above all power and might. Do we ask something which even natural law would seem to hinder? God already has done something in His resurrection which is superior to all law for that is what "dominion" means. Are we confronted with imposing names and despised by human pride? We are sitting side by side with one who is exalted above every name that is named both in this world and that which is to come. Indeed, the whole economy of human life, the whole system of providence is a framework for the accomplishment of God's purposes for His redeemed people. Nations rise and fall, human society exists, great cities swarm with their inhabitants and move with the mighty currents of commerce and social life. All the events of the great world as they pass are but movements of Christ's mighty hand, primarily designed for those who immediately take part in them, but ultimately for the good of His church and the building up of His kingdom; and men and nations are but puppets in the hands of our anointed King, whom He uses for His wise purposes even when they are fulfilling their own pleasure, and then drops them when He pleases. After the resurrection of Christ, and in view of His enthronement there is nothing we need fear to claim according to this mighty measure, as part of the riches of our inheritance.

VI. CHRIST HIMSELF

We read in Romans 15: "According to Christ Jesus." This is the highest of all standards, higher even that His resurrection, ascension and glory. As He is, so shall we be when He appears, but "As he is so are we," even here. "Ye are not of the world even as I am not of the world." "Love one another as I have loved you"; "As I live by the Father: so he that eateth me, even he shall live by me." "As thou hast sent me into the world, even so have I sent them into the world." "When he shall appear, we shall be like him; for we shall see him as he is." Such are some of the touches of heavenly light which reveal our identity with Jesus and unfold the mystery of His life in us. Not only is He our example, but He is our life. Miniatures of Christ, God expects us to be, receiving and reflecting Him in all His fullness, our life His life, our love His love, His riches ours. We represent Him, we dwell among men not as citizens of earth, but dead to our old citizenship and walking like Him as if we had been sent specially from heaven on a mission from another world.

Beloved, is Christ our Pattern, our Type, our living Head, our Divine Standard and Measure? Are we determined to have nothing less and to be nothing less than even as He? Shall we cease to copy men, and follow only Him!

And even though we often are conscious of very imperfect resemblance to the Great Original, are we still holding our standard as high as Christ? I have often noticed the artists in the great gallery copying the paintings of the masters. I have sometimes come back weeks afterwards and found them still working on the copy of some great painting. Their work was not complete, but their copy was, and while it hung upon the wall with its pefect form and tints their copy was constantly reaching closer approximation to the great object lesson. But if they had begun to copy the works of the artists around them or to complete the picture from their own recollection or conception of it, it would have soon become a cheap and worthless daub.

So let us always keep our eye upon the heavenly standard and be satisfied with nothing less than "according to Christ Jesus." Sometimes in kindergarten schools a picture is held before the children for a little and then it is removed and they are required to tell from memory some of its features. Then it is held again and they are again required to tell or draw some of the features that they have noticed and marked until, at length, the whole object lesson is imprinted like a copy upon their minds. So God holds Jesus before us and bids us, not only follow our conception of Him, or the copies we see in others, but again and again contemplate the Original and hold Him constantly in view that even our conception of Christ shall be ever corrected, enlarged, vivified, until it shall be transformed to our inmost being, not only as the Pattern but as the very life of our life.

"Christ men," as one has said, "are the men God wants today." It would not hurt if this word became coined into Christian phraseology, and its meaning stamped upon all our life. A poor heathen Kroo boy came on board a ship, hundreds of miles from the Congo and finding a party of missionaries going up the river, eagerly sought an interview with them and sent a message by them to one of the missionaries in the far interior. "Tell him," he said in his rude speech, "that when I left him two years ago I promised to be Christ's man. Tell him that I am Christ's man still." Rude and simple as the heathen conception was it was the truest and the highest that mortal thought can reach. It is God's own divine measure of Christian life, to be a "Christ man," living, loving, trusting, serving, suffering, overcoming, "according to Christ Jesus."

VII. According to the Power That Worketh in Us

"Now unto him that is able to do exceeding abundantly above all that we ask or think, according to the power that worketh in us" (Eph. 3:20).

"Whereunto I also labour, striving according to his working, which worketh in me mightily" (Col. 1:29).

"According to the working whereby he is able to subdue all things unto himself" (Phil. 3:21).

In these passages we have God's present working referred to in two directions, namely, in the believer's heart and in the sphere of providence and government. The one must ever keep pace with the other. God does work mightily in the forces around us, but we must allow Him to work within us or all the might of His providence shall be ineffectual for us. "He is able to do exceeding abundantly," but it must be wrought in us. It is "according to the power that worketh in us." All the forces of that mighty engine in the factory yonder are limited and measured by the attachment of the little pulley of each particular machine. It can drive a hundred printing presses if they are in contact, but its power is according to the measure in which each one will receive it and co-operate. God is waiting to work in each of us, indeed He is already working up to the full measure of our yieldedness, and we may have all which we are willing to have inwrought in our own being. The Holy Spirit is always in advance of us, pressing us on to more than we have yet wholly received and we may be very sure that according to the measure of His inward pressure will always be the external workings of God's almighty hand. Whenever we find the wheels within motion we may be very sure that the wheels of providence are moving in accord, even to the utmost bounds of the universe and to the utmost limits of God's almighty power and supreme authority.

Let us then yield to the power that worketh in us to its full measure. Let our being be responsive to its slightest touch, so responsive that, like the Æolian harp, it will answer to the faintest breath of the Holy Spirit as He moves upon the chords of our inmost being.

VIII. According to Our Faith

"According to thy faith be it unto thee" was Christ's great law of healing and blessing in His earthly ministry. This was what He meant when He said "with what measure ye mete it shall be measured to you again." All these mighty measures that we have been holding up are limited by the measures that we bring. God deals out His heavenly treasures to us in these glorious vessels, but each of us must bring our drinking cup and according to its measure we shall be filled. But even the measure of our faith may be a divine one. Thank God, the little cup has become enlarged through the grace of Jesus, until from its bottom there flows a pipe into the great ocean, and if that connection is kept open we shall find that our cup is as large as the ocean and never can be drained to the bottom. For He has said to us "Have the faith of God," and surely this is an illimitable measure.

A few weeks ago a noble band of missionaries landed upon the coast of Sierra Leone filled with faith and holy enthusiasm. Before many days however three of their number had fallen victims to the dreadful African fever. Shortly afterwards one of these dear brothers wrote to us a very touching and wonderful message. He said that on his way across the Atlantic he had been led to see the truth of divine healing and had taken the Lord Jesus as his healer. Soon after, the death of these friends came upon him like a bewildering shock and for a few hours his faith seemed to be wholly paralyzed. Then he threw himself at the feet of Jesus and to his surprise there came upon him such a baptism of rest and confidence, with which he seemed to have nothing to do, that he rose not only comforted, but so established in His confidence, so assured that the Lord was his healer and keeper that he had no fear even of the failure of his faith, but was able to say with humble and holy confidence that come what might he would trust the Lord alone, and was confident that his life and faith would be upheld until his work was done. His old faith had died, and out of its grave had come the faith of God. His little drinking cup had broken, and all the water had leaked out. But lo! A hand divine had opened through that broken cup a connection with that heavenly fountain, and henceforth his cup was not only full but full forevermore with all the fullness of God. He had passed out of himself into Christ, and was now able to meet the immeasurable promises with a trust as measureless and divine.

So let us, beloved, rise into the fullness of Jesus and sweetly

> "Find His fullness round our incompleteness,
> Round our restlessness, His rest."

X

Spiritual Growth

"But grow in grace and in the knowledge of our Lord and Savior Jesus Christ" [2 Peter 3:18].

I HAVE heard of a little boy being found by his mother in one of the garden beds with his feet buried in the soil, and standing beside a tall sunflower, to which he was eagerly looking up. When his mother asked him what it all meant, he said that he was trying to grow to be a man, and wanted to be as tall as the sunflower. How truly has our Master said of all our struggles to grow taller, "Which of you by taking thought can add one cubit to his stature?" All the little fellow's stretching did not increase his height. No doubt his mother told him to go inside and eat a good hearty supper, and day by day drink plenty of fresh milk and eat his meals with heartiness, and run about and play for wholesome exercise and be a happy, thoughtless child, and thus he would grow to be a man without trying. His desire to grow would not really help him to grow unless he took the proper means.

It is just so in our spiritual life. Fretting and straining will not enlarge our spiritual manhood. God has Himself revealed the secret of growth, and it is not very different from the mother's counsel to her little boy.

Let us look at some principles of spiritual progress.

I. The Relation of Spiritual Growth to Sanctification

The apostle who has given us our text had already laid down the principles of spiritual growth in the opening chapter of his epistle with great fullness and marvelous clearness and power. There is no single paragraph in the

Scriptures which more profoundly unfolds the depths and heights of Christian life than the first eleven verses of the first chapter of 2nd Peter. And the very point we are now referring to is made perfectly plain in these verses. The fifth verse is an injunction to grow in grace, but the preceding verses give us the standpoint from which this growth is to start. It is nothing less than the experience of sanctification. The persons to whom this is addressed are recognized as having already "escaped the corruption that is in the world through lust," and having already "become partakers of the divine nature."

These two facts constitute the whole of sanctification. It is that experience by which we become united to Christ in so divine and personal a sense that we become partakers of His nature, and the very person of Christ, through the Holy Ghost, comes to dwell in our hearts, and by His indwelling becomes to us the substance and support of our spiritual life. The converted soul is a human spirit born from above by the power of the Holy Spirit. The sanctified soul is that human spirit wholly yielded to and wholly possessed and occupied by God's indwelling presence, so as to be able to say, "Not I, but Christ liveth in me." The effect of this is to deliver from "the corruption that is in the world through lust." God's indwelling excludes the power of sin and evil desire, which is just what the word lust means. The Greek tenses here leave no room to doubt the question of time and the order of events. This deliverance from corruption precedes the command to grow, and is the very ground of that command. For the word translated "besides this," as Alford so happily shows, means something entirely different, namely, "for this very reason," that is, because God hath provided for our sanctification, and imparted to us His nature and delivered us from the power of sin, for this very reason we are to grow.

It is very evident, therefore, that we do not grow into sanctification, but grow from sanctification into maturity. This corresponds exactly with the description of the growth of Christ Himself in the opening of the gospel of Luke. "The child grew and waxed strong in spirit, filled with wisdom: and the grace of God was upon him." Surely no one will dare to say that He grew into sanctification. He was sanctified from the very first. But He was a sanctified *child* and grew into manhood. And so still later, in Luke 2: 52, it is added that, at the age of twelve years, "Jesus increased in wisdom and stature, and in favour with God and man."

And so the same Christ is formed in each of us; is formed as a babe and grows, as He did on earth, into maturity in our spiritual life, and we grow into a closer union with Him, and a more habitual and intimate dependence upon Him for all our life and actions.

Beloved, have we come to the starting point of spiritual growth by receiving Christ as our indwelling sanctifier and life?

II. THE RELATION OF GROWTH TO THE PROVISIONS AND RESOURCES OF DIVINE GRACE

The same beautiful passage brings this out also in great fullness and definiteness. "According as his divine power hath given unto us all things that pertain unto life and godliness, through the knowledge of him that hath called us to glory and virtue. Whereby are given unto us exceeding great and precious promises." Here we are taught that God hath provided all the resources necessary for a holy and mature Christian life. These resources are provided for us through the graces and virtues of our Lord Jesus Christ, which we are called to receive and share. "He hath called us," not to our glory and virtue, but "to his glory and virtue." It is the same thought which the same apostle expresses in his first epistle, 2:9, "That ye should shew forth the excellencies of him who hath called you out of darkness into his marvellous light." Not, "the praises of him," which is obviously a bad translation, but "the excellencies." We are to display the excellencies of Jesus to the world, or, as it is here, "The glory and virtue of Jesus." He clothes us with His character and in His garments, and we are to exhibit them to men and to angels. And these provisions of grace are brought within our reach through all "the exceeding great and precious promises," which we may claim and turn into heavenly currency for every needed blessing.

This is the conception of Christian life given in the first chapter of the gospel of John, in that wonderful little expression "grace for grace." That is to say, every grace that we need to exercise already exists in Christ, and may be transferred into our life from Him, as we "receive of his fullness, even grace for grace." Up in yonder mount Moses was called to see and study a model of the Tabernacle, corresponding in a higher degree to the models which you may see in the Patent Office in Washington of all the different machines that have been patented and built. A few weeks later the same Tabernacle might be seen going up piecemeal in the valley below, and, when completed, was an exact facsimile of the other shown to Moses in the mount; for God's explicit command was, "See, saith he, that thou make all things according to the pattern shewed to thee in the mount." Corresponding to this is the tabernacle which God is building in each of our lives. It is just as heavenly a structure as the other and far more important, and is meant to be, as it is, the dwelling-place of God. It, too, has its model in the mount, and we may see, by the eye of faith, the model of our life, the pattern, the plan of all the graces which we exemplify and the life which is to be built up, worked out, and established. All the material for our spiritual building are there now, already provided, and the whole design fully wrought out in the purpose of God and the provisions of His grace. But we have to take these resources and materials moment by moment, step by step, and transfer them into our lives. We have not to make the graces ourselves, but take them, wear them, live them, and exhibit them. "Of his fulness we receive grace for grace," His graces for our graces, His love for our love, His trust for our trust, His power for our strength.

Over in an English factory you can find numerous models of iron cottages, composed of hundreds of sections screwed together, and standing just as they would appear when erected on their permanent site. The purchaser from a distant colony, where wood is scarce and metal has to be used instead, comes along and purchases one of these cottages, and orders it to be shipped to Australia, with the understanding that it shall correspond in every particular to the model in the London yard. The order is fulfilled, and a few months later you may see the identical facsimile standing in a pleasant lawn in Melbourne or Sidney, or a few weeks sooner you may see the sections arrive piece by piece, and the different pieces screwed together until the building is complete, and corresponds in every particular to the London model. All the materials have been sent from the distant city, and the structure reared according to the model, piece for piece. This will illustrate what John meant by "grace for grace." Christ has, in Himself, the pattern of your life and mine, and all the materials. Our part is simply to receive, live out and exemplify them before the world.

III. RELATION OF SPIRITUAL GROWTH TO OUR OWN RESPONSIBILITY AND EFFORTS

While it is true, on the one hand, that all the resources are divinely provided, this does not justify, on our part, a spirit of passive negligence, but summons us all the more to diligence and earnestness in pressing forward in our spiritual career. And so the apostle adds, after this strongly emphasized enumeration of the resources of God's grace, "Giving all diligence, add to your faith," etc. There is to be no languid leaning upon God's grace, no dreamy fatalism, based upon His almighty purpose and power, but a strenuous and unceasing energy on our part in meeting Him with the co-operation of our faith, vigilance and obedience. In fact, the very provisions of God's grace are made, by the apostle, the ground of His exhortation to give earnest attention to this matter. For this very reason, that is, because God has so abundantly provided for us, and is so mightily working in our lives, and hearts and developing us from the power of sin, for this very reason, "Add to your faith," etc.

It is the same thought which Paul has expressed in Philippians, "Work out your own salvation with fear and trembling. For it is God which worketh in you to will and to do of his good pleasure." This does not mean that we are to work for our salvation, for we are represented as already saved, otherwise it could not be "our own salvation." But it is yet in embryo and infancy, an inward principle of life which must be worked out into its full development and maturity in every part of our life, and to this we are "to give all diligence," a diligence indeed, which often reaches the extent of "fear and trembling," a holy and solemn sense of responsibility to make the most of our spiritual resources and opportunities, because "it is God that worketh in us." It is as if, with the finger of solemn warning raised, He were standing and looking into our eyes and saying, "God has come. The Almighty has taken this matter in hand. The Eternal Jehovah has undertaken the work, therefore, mind what you do! Let there be no laxness, no negligence, and no failure on your part to meet Him and afford Him the utmost opportunity to fulfill in you all the good pleasure of His will, and the accomplishment of His high and mighty purpose for your soul."

In a Sunday school lesson some time ago, there was a very solemn thought, whose most impressive point has perhaps escaped the thought of some of us. It is in connection with the parable of the pounds, and the thought we refer to is the obvious truth there unfolded, that to every servant is given at the beginning of his spiritual life, an equal measure of spiritual resource, and that the difference in the issues of human lives is not to be found in the unequal measure of grace and power afforded from on high, but in the unequal measure in which they have improved the power given. One pound is given to each servant, but in the end, one servant has so traded with his pound that it has grown to ten, while his neighbor has the same little pound wrapped up in a napkin, unchanged, unimproved. The difference lies wholly in the diligence of the two men. The one "giving all diligence" added to his faith virtue, knowledge, temperance. The other simply tried to keep what he got and probably took excellent care of it, wrapping it in a costly handkerchief may be, or putting it into a secret drawer or worthy place, but doing nothing to increase it. "The manifestation of the Spirit is given to every man," the apostle says, "to profit withal." This expression, "to profit," carries the same idea with it as the trading in the parable of the pounds and the "all diligence" of Peter's epistle.

Beloved are we "giving all diligence" to make the most

of God's divine resources, of "the exceeding great and precious promises," of "the divine nature," within us?

IV. THE RELATION OF THE VARIOUS DETAILS AND THE RESPECTIVE GRACES OF OUR CHRISTIAN LIFE

The verse employed to describe our spiritual progress is a very unusual one and full of exquisite suggestiveness. It is a musical figure, and we all know that there is nothing that so perfectly expresses the idea of harmony and adjustment as music. Paraphrased into the English meaning of the figure the passage might thus be read, "Add to your faith, virtue, knowledge, temperance," etc., just as in a perfect musical harmony one note is added to another and one chord to another until the majestic Hallelujah Chorus swells to heaven without a discordant part or measure wanting.

In the Greek national festivals it was customary for some prominent and gifted individual to get up a chorus or special musical entertainment, and the one to whom this high trust was committed was called the *Choregos.* From this our word choir has been derived. He was really the choirmaster and his business was to combine together the voices, the instruments and the musical compositions in such a manner as to produce the most perfect effect and the most complete harmony. So the Greek verb based on this word, *"Epichorego,"* just means to combine together as a musical harmony, or as a choirmaster would combine the notes, the instruments, the voices and all the parts in a splendid performance. This is the beautiful verb imperfectly translated. A dry figure of arithmetic is unhappily substituted for a suggestive musical metaphor.

Perhaps we have already anticipated the fine thought lying back of this figure, viz: that God wishes our Christian growth to be like the growth of a sublime oratorio, a growth in which all the parts are so blended and the entire effect so harmonious that our life will be like a heavenly song or a Hallelujah Chorus. Faith is the melody, but to this is added all the other parts, courage, which reaches the high tenor, temperance, perhaps the medium alto, patience, the deep bass, and knowledge, godliness, and love, the song itself, to which all the music is but the accompaniment. It is easy to grow in one direction and to be strong in one peculiarity, but only the grace of God and the power of the divine nature within can enable us to grow up to Him in all things, "unto the measure of the stature of the fulness of Christ." It is one thing to have faith and courage, but it is another thing to have that blended with temperance and love. It is one thing to have self-restraint, but it is another thing to have it combined with knowledge. It is one thing to have brotherly kindness, but it is quite another to have charity to all men. It is one thing to have godliness but it is another to have it in perfect adjustment with love. It is the harmony with all the parts which constitutes the perfection of the song and the completeness of the Christian life.

Beloved, perhaps God has educated you in each of the graces but He is now educating you in the blending of these graces in perfect proportion, so that your love will be rendered mellow and like a perfectly proportioned face, not so marked in any of its single features as in the whole expression of the countenance. Indeed the most beautiful faces are sometimes so proportioned that we can scarcely remember a single feature, and perhaps the best musical compositions are those which leave the simplest effects and are less striking for any particular measure than for the exquisite sweetness and simplicity of the whole. This is the heavenly meaning brought out in the preposition "*in*" all through this progression. It is not *add* to your faith courage, but "*in* your faith courage, knowledge, temperance, etc." It is in the intermingling and the tempering of one grace with another that the power of the whole consists. It is the addition of courage along with the faith which renders the faith effectual. It is the addition of self-restraint along with patience which keeps its from becoming fanaticism, and zeal without knowledge. It is in the quality of temperance and self-control combined with knowledge that the elements of discretion and wisdom are developed. But self-control and self-denial need patience to save them from being transitory outbursts and to give them permanence and stability. All these qualities without godliness would leave us on a low plane, but this lifts them all to heaven and makes them all a living sacrifice upon the altar of His glory. But even godliness alone would leave us narrow and cold, and so God requires of us the inner linking with our brethren and the culture of these social qualities which bring us into loving fellowship with one another and lift us out of ourselves into brotherly kindness, that is the love of the brethren, the love of Christ's people. And yet even this would not be complete if the circle were not widened far beyond the range of Christ's people and our brethren in the Lord, to comprehend the whole world in the sweep of a charity which can love even as God loves, the unworthy, the unattractive and even those that hate us and repel us.

It is very beautiful to notice the fine shades of holy character which the New Testament expresses. For example, what a multitude of words the Holy Spirit has given us for the various forms of love and patience. Here are some of them: love, charity, brotherly kindness, tenderness, meekness, longsuffering, patience, forbearance, unity, peace, courtesy, gentleness, considering one another, in honor preferring one another, kindly affectioned one to another, etc. They are like so many fine shades of color, all of the same class, yet no two exactly the same. Thus God is tempering our lives and this is a very large part of Christian growth.

It is said that a great sculptor was visited by a friend twice, at an interval of several months. The friend was astonished to find that his work seemed no further on. "What have you been doing?" "Why," he said, "I have been touching this feature, rounding that, raising that." "Why, but these are all trifles, mere touches!" "Yes," said the artist, "but these make perfection and perfection is no trifle." It is an old story but a spiritual lesson which is very far from worn out. God keeps us sometimes years learning a few touches and heavenliness, which constitutes the difference between the image of Christ and the blundered and broken image of an imperfect man.

V. THE RELATION OF GROWTH TO OUR SECURITY AND STEADFASTNESS IN CHRISTIAN LIFE

It is not a matter of personal preference whether we shall grow or not. It is a matter of vital necessity, for only thus can we be kept from retrograding. This the apostle hints in our text, "Beware lest ye also, being led away with the error of the wicked, fall from your own stedfastness. But grow in grace, and in the knowledge of our Lord and Saviour Jesus Christ." Growth is the remedy for declension and we must ever grow or go backward. So in 2 Peter 1:1, the same truth is expounded. "If ye do these things ye shall never fall: He that lacketh these things is blind, and cannot see afar off, and hath forgotten that he was purged from his old sins." That is the very experience of conversion—it fades away and becomes but a dim recollection unless we press on to deeper and higher things.

Alas! have we not all sometimes seen men truly and wonderfully converted and much used of God for the conversion even of others, and yet men who refused to go on to higher experiences, and sometimes even have scouted the doctrine and experience of sanctification as an affectation or fanaticism. Alas! The day came when even their experience of conversion faded, at least for a time, and they were plunged in some deep and bitter fall to compel them to see the need of something higher. It is not possible for us to remain with safety in any stereotyped experience. Indeed, it is necessary for us to grow with an accelerated motion and to make more rapid progress the longer we continue in the Christian life.

And so we have a very strong figure even in this passage expressing this thought. The word translated "abound" in our version, in the Greek is "multiply." "If these things be in you, and multiply, they make you that ye shall neither be barren nor unfruitful in the knowledge of our Lord Jesus Christ." Let us not fail to notice the striking antithesis of the "add" in verse 3, and the "multiply" of verse 8. We all know in arithmetic the difference between addition and multiplication. The addition of nine to nine makes eighteen, but the multiplication of nine times nine reverses the figures and makes eighty-one, or nearly five times as much. Everything depends upon the size of the multiplier. In the spiritual arithmetic the multiplier is God and infinitely higher than the highest digits of human calculation. God simply takes the surrendered heart and unites Himself with it, and the result is as many times greater than itself as God is greater than man.

Beloved, shall we meet God's expectation and provision and press on from grace to grace and from grace to glory?

VI. THE RELATION OF GROWTH TO REWARD

The apostle carries on the thought to the sublime consummation when the struggles and trials of time shall all have passed and we shall be entering the eternal port and coming into the eternal issues of our present lives. Then no struggle will be regarded as too severe, no self-denial will be regretted, no toilsome patient victory will be remembered as too trying, but these very things will constitute the exquisite joy and recompense of our eternal homecoming. "For so," he says, "an entrance shall be ministered unto you abundantly into the everlasting kingdom of our Lord and Saviour Jesus Christ." How it lights up this whole passage with a wondrous glory to remember that the Greek word used here to describe our entrance into the kingdom is the very same Greek word used with respect to the "adding" to our faith virtue, knowledge, temperance, godliness, and all the train of heavenly graces. It is the beautiful metaphor of the *"choregos."* It is not that an abundant entrance merely shall be ministered unto us, but the idea is that a whole chorus of heavenly voices and harmonies will sing us home, and that we shall enter like warriors returning in triumphal procession from a hard-won and glorious victory. It is not merely that a chorus will meet us, but it is the very same choir that we ourselves gathered around us in our earthly conflict. The graces, the virtues, the victories, the triumphs of patience and love that we won and perhaps had quite forgotten will all be waiting yonder like troops of angels, and all shall gather round us and fit into the chorus of joy that shall celebrate our homecoming.

Sometimes God has given us a little taste on earth of this ecstatic joy, when some ministry of love that we had long ago forgotten comes back to our recollection through the friend whom we had been the means of saving, or some word or deed is recalled by the testimony of one to whom we were made a blessing through an act of self-denial or faithfulness; and we find, a quarter of a century afterwards, that the little service has been traveling round the world and blessing hundreds on the way. We are melted into grateful wonder and adoring praise.

But these are but approximations of what it will be then, when all that we have been permitted to suffer and do for Jesus will be found awaiting us on the threshold of glory, and shall usher her in triumphal procession into the eternal kingdom of our Lord and Saviour Jesus Christ. Oh how we shall rejoice that we were permitted once to suffer and sacrifice for Jesus! Oh, how some will wish that they might have once more the opportunity of winning such a welcome and gaining such a great reward. Beloved, nothing that we gain for God can ever be lost. Oh, may the Master help us, "giving all diligence," to make the most of life and all its opportunities and resources of grace and lay up for ourselves treasures on high which shall never fade away.

XI

Enlarged Work

1. Attempt great things for God.
2. Expect great things from God.

"Enlarge the place of thy tent" [Isa. 54:2].

ABOUT one hundred years ago a humble Baptist preacher stood in an English pulpit and announced this text at the opening of what was perhaps the first Missionary Convention of modern times. He then proposed the two following divisions as the themes of his discourse: (1) Attempt great things for God; and (2) expect great things from God. And then from these two propositions, themselves inspiring enough to impel the whole missionary movement, he proceeded to preach a sermon which became the watchword of the greatest Christian movement, since Apostolic days. That was the birthday of modern missions. Soon he himself was a missionary in Calcutta, and today an army of missionaries is girdling the world and about to multiply more and more every year until the Master comes. The preacher had been one of those whom the Lord delights to use, one of the weak things, and the things that are despised. A humble cobbler, he had supported himself by toiling all day long at his last, but while his hands were busy, his heart was out upon the world, and his eyes were often upon the maps that lined the walls of his workshop, and the calculations and plans for the world's evangelization. Deep down in his heart had grown up a mighty faith for the lost millions of mankind, and his great sermon was but the outbreaking of the pent-up fires that had long been burning in his breast. It was the voice of God to his generation. It is the voice of God to another generation, the generation of today. It is the voice of God to us, beloved. Fresh from the hallowed influences that have so deeply moved our hearts and blessed so many here, God is pointing to a world where a thousand millions still are lost, and saying to us— "Enlarge the place of thy tent, and let them stretch forth the curtains of thine habitations: spare not, lengthen thy cords, and strengthen thy stakes; For thou shalt break forth on the right hand and on the left; and thy seed shall inherit the Gentiles, and make the desolate cities to be inhabited. Fear not; for thou shalt not be ashamed: neither be thou confounded; for thou shalt not be put to shame: for thou shalt forget the shame of thy youth and shalt not remember the reproach of thy widowhood any more. For thy Maker is thine husband; the Lord of hosts is his name; and thy Redeemer the Holy One of Israel; The God of the whole earth shall he be called."

Three thoughts are here suggested.

I. ENLARGEMENT

God's plan for all His work is to begin in feebleness and expand and develop to maturity. He first makes a perfect sample and then multiplies it. So the work He has done for us is but a sample of what He can do, and wants to do for all the world. The blessing that has filled and thrilled our hearts these past days, may be multiplied as many times as there are cities in the world, and reproduced wherever there are hungry hearts to fill and messengers to tell of the grace and the fullness of Jesus. That gospel of the Saviour's fullness that has filled your heart can fill a thousand million hearts. That faith which has brought you deliverance can deliver all the captives of the great oppressor and set the whole world free. That humble work which has grown up out of "a handful of corn on the top of the mountains" can become a mighty forest on all the mountains and "shake like Lebanon, and they of the city flourish like the grass of the field."

God has simply been making samples, but He can multiply them by millions. Will we let Him use us for their reproduction, for they are multiplied by reproduction. They are not made as the machines in yonder factory, but they grow as seeds multiply, as yonder geraniums by culturings, as that oak by the seeds it drops into the ground, or that single grain of wheat that sometimes sends up twenty stalks from a single seed, and each stalk bears half a hundred seeds. God has given us in this blessed work a gospel so full that it needs a world for its field. He is showing us the plan of a Christian church, that is much more than an association of congenial friends to listen once a week to an intellectual and musical entertainment and carry on by proxy a mechanism of Christian work; but rather a church than can be at once the mother and the home of every form of help and blessing which Jesus came to give to lost and suffering men, the birthplace and the home of souls, the fountain of healing and cleansing, the sheltering home for the orphan and distressed, the school for the culture and training of God's children, the armory where they are equipped for the battle of the Lord and the army which fights those battles in His name. Such a centre of life and power Christ wants in every centre of population in this sad and sinful world.

The figure of enlargement is that of a tent; its curtains are to be stretched forth and its cords are to be lengthened. These curtains are surely the promises and provisions of the Gospel, and they will stretch as wide as the needs of human lives and the multitudes that seek their shelter. The cords are cords of prayer, cords of faith, cords of love, cords of holy effort and service. He bids us lengthen the cords of prayer. Let us ask more, but let the strands of faith be as long and strong. Let us believe more fully, more firmly, and for a wider circle than we have dared before. Let the cords of love be lengthened until we shall draw men to Christ with the very cords of our hearts. Let our efforts for His kingdom reach a wider circle. Let each of us make the world our parish, and as the Bride of the Lamb realize that all that concerns our Lord's kingdom concerns our hearts, "For thy Maker is thine husband; the Lord of hosts is his name; . . . the God of the whole earth shall he be called."

God has committed to our trust the gospel in its fullness. Let us never rest until in all its fullness it is known in every hamlet of this great land and in every land and tongue.

And we must lengthen the cords of our liberality. The Lord is asking for millions today to spread His gospel in its fullness over the world, and we to whom this full gospel has been such a blessing are especially called to take it as our trust for Him and send it everywhere. The world is open today and the workers are being prepared as never before, men and women full of faith and the Holy Ghost. Never was there a time when a little money would go so far is spreading Christ's Word. Less than ten millions today would evangelize all the world before the close of the century. (Written in 1890—*Editor.*)

When I think of the opportunity of using money for God today, I could almost envy the men who have the opportunities of successful business. God is going to send very large amounts into the treasuries of consecrated work, and if we are but true to this trust we shall yet see tens of millions spent in sending the fourfold gospel to every corner of the globe.

II. CONSOLIDATION

But the wider our work the stronger it must be at the centre. And therefore as the cords are lengthened the stakes must also be strengthened. What are these stakes?

1. Surely God's Word is the first. The more widespread the work God gives us to do the more important is it that we be true to the great standard of truth, the Bible and the gospel of Jesus Christ. This is the day of new theologies and loose views of evangelical truth. More sacredly than ever does the Master require us to stand faithful to the cross of Jesus Christ, the doctrine of man's sin and ruin, the great atonement, the inspiration of the Holy Scriptures, the person and work of the Holy Ghost, and the certainties of future retribution and reward. Thank God we do not have to resort to the novelties of rationalism to attract the multitudes. Give them the Living Bread, the atoning blood, the old and ever new story of Jesus and His love.

2. Personal holiness. This is the next safeguard of the Lord's work. God cannot trust an unsanctified people or an unconsecrated man with much service for Him. Poor Jonah is sure to mar his most sucessful work with a touch of himself. The more God entrusts to our hands the more humbly let us lie at His feet and the more faithfully use our trust for His glory. God grant us wisdom to see to it that all who bear the vessels of the Lord are clean. So shall He give us the world itself for our inheritance.

3. The spirit of self-sacrifice. No work can ever be glorious without the martyr spirit. Luxury is killing the churches today, and the only remedy for it is the red blood of sacrifice. Great faith and great sacrifice will always be found together. This must be the spirit of this work if it is to cover the world. We must be willing to endure hardness as good soldiers of Jesus Christ. We must be indifferent to popularity, and human praise or blame, we must be willing to live with great simplicity and rigid economy, we must be willing to be misunderstood

and persecuted, we must be glad to be the companions of the lowly and despised, we must gladly face toil, hardship and even death, and count all things but loss for Christ and His kingdom. Such a people only can possess the world for Christ and such soldiers shall march to world-wide victory while the splendid brigades of rank and luxury shall fail in the day of battle and prove but a splendid pageant and a dress parade.

God give us the spirit of Scriptural faith, personal consecration, and true self-sacrifice, and then He can give us the world for Christ.

The figure of the tent suggests the idea of constant vicissitudes and humility. This is no proud architectural pile but a simple tent, ever changing and oft taken down and moved forward. It is the figure of the changing wilderness, the pilgrim life and constant movement. This is not our rest. This is no place for great cathedrals and splendid establishments, and ecclesiastical states, but continual advance and ceaseless aggression. It is to be feared that splendid churches have been the greatest curse of the church. As long as the early Christians met in humble upper rooms, they had the power of God and godliness, but when they began to imitate the splendor of the world and vie with the architecture of imperial palaces and heathen temples, the Holy Spirit took His flight, and the world and the devil became paramount. The days of the Jewish tabernacle were better days than those of Solomon's temple. The beginning of this work was in a humble tent; let us never forget the tent spirit or lose the pilgrim spirit. "Enlarge the place of thy tent." He does not say get a temple, but a bigger tent. Lord help us to enlarge but never leave our tents.

III. DIVINE RESOURCES

"For thy Maker is thine husband; the Lord of Hosts is his name, the God of the whole earth shall he be called."

This is the secret of it all. We have back of us one who has infinite resources, and He is not only our King and our Friend, He is our Husband. He has given us all His heart and all His glory, and He will surely give us all the world for our dowry and our inheritance. This is the secret of successful work, to know Christ in this blissful and intimate relation, and to receive our work, by virtue of our union with Him, as the very fruit of our marriage with the King of kings. So may He reveal Himself to us all, and then, as His very bride, standing at the threshold of His home and inviting in His lost and wandering children, it shall be true of us, "The Spirit and the bride say come," and the world will come to Him.

"How knowest thou whether thou be come to the kingdom for such a time as this?" Like Esther on Ahasuerus' throne, we have been called to the kingdom that we might use our place of right and power to save the world. God help us so to win them back to our beloved Husband, so to bear them for Him as His very children and ours, that "the God of the whole earth shall he be called."

It has been the experience of some of God's children, and it was mine, to be called by His Spirit, in years of loneliness and sorrow, to learn very deeply the Song of Solomon in its true spiritual significance, and then, in this deep, sweet love-life with Christ, to be led into precious service for Him, and to find the life filled with most gracious fruitfulness and blessing. O beloved, He is calling you to His bosom and then to His work, "Hearken, O daughter, and consider, and incline thine ear; forget also thine own people, and thy father's house; So shall the king greatly desire thy beauty: for he is thy Lord; and worship thou him." And then, "Instead of thy fathers shall be thy children, whom thou mayest make princes in the earth."

THE PURSUIT OF GOD by A.W. Tozer is as contemporary as today's newspaper. And A.W. Tozer is as incisive as any writer can be. Tozer fans will welcome this new edition of an inspirational classic. 128 pages, paper, $1.95.

CHARLES BOWEN: "PAUL BUNYAN" OF THE CANADIAN WEST by W. Phillip Keller. Charles Bowen feared neither noose nor submarine. In Keller's unusual true account he survives both to carry the gospel to Canada's Western frontier. (Originally entitled **Bold Under God**, Moody Press.) 141 pages, paper, $1.95.

THE TAMING OF MOLLY by Molly Clark is the author's own account of how God came into her life and changed her. A story of spiritual and physical healing, "backsliding," and progress. Humorous, warm, and helpful. 96 pages, paper, $1.50.

THE SHEPHERD'S PSALM and other true accounts edited by Eric Mills. Exciting insights into one of the world's favorite pieces of literature (Psalm 23) plus "The Flask that Wouldn't Break," "A Broken Home and a Broken Heart" and more. (Formerly entitled **Preachers, Priests, and Critters**.) 93 pages, paper, $1.95.

BEYOND THE TANGLED MOUNTAIN by Douglas C. Percy is an authentic African novel by an award-winning Canadian author. From his pen spins a fascinating web of missionary heroism, romance, tension and tragedy. Douglas Percy is one of the "best" on Africa. First time in paperback. 158 pages, paper, $1.95.

TREASURES IN HEAVEN by Beatrice Sundbo is a warm, human look at how the author faced the deaths of four of her family, then her own death. Inspiring and triumphant. 96 pages, paper, $1.75.

CRISIS AT 9:25 by Barry Moore is a collection of hard-hitting messages by an international evangelist from London, Canada. Pointed and provocative. 95 pages, paper, $1.75.

CHOCOLATE CAKE AND ONIONS....WITH LOVE by Marilynne E. Foster is a collection of recipes that she has discovered in her own use to be tasty and easy to prepare. The love comes in selected excerpts from various writings on the theme of love. 96 pages, paper, spiral spine, $1.95.

TO YOUR KITCHEN...WITH LOVE by Barbara Schaefer. This beautiful, spiral-bound cookbook is a delightful collection of tasty recipes compiled by a missionary mother for her bride-to-be daughter. Timely devotional thoughts sprinkled throughout. Diet section included. 117 pages, paper, $3.95.

BORN AGAIN: WHAT IT REALLY MEANS by Alain Choiquier. This old term, once muttered in embarrassment, has now invaded Madison Avenue. Its true meaning is admirably explained by French preacher Choiquier. 400,000 in print in French, now for the first time in English. 51 pages, paper, shrinkwrap pack of six for $4.75, the price of five. Not sold separately by the publisher.

SPEAKING WITH OTHER TONGUES by T.J. McCrossan. Sub-titled "Sign or Gift—Which?" this book is by a former instructor in Greek at the University of Manitoba, a Christian well able to dissect and explain this controversial issue. Vigorous, relevant, and helpful. 68 pages, paper, $1.75.

ALIVE AND FREE by Marney Patterson. This Anglican evangelist has come up with another Horizon title which reveals the heart of his international message and ministry. Pictures throughout. 160 pages, paper, $2.50.

I WISH YOU COULD MEET MY MOM AND DAD by Tom Allen. What makes a 23-year-old son brag on his mom and dad? And why do his nine brothers and sisters feel the very same way? Humorous, helpful and inspiring. 121 pages, trade size, paper, $2.95.

UFOs: SATANIC TERROR by Basil Tyson. Around the world an estimated six UFOs are sighted every hour. Tyson's explanation is both startling and impressive. 116 pages, paper, $1.95.

DAM BREAK IN GEORGIA by K. Neill Foster with Eric Mills. At 1:30 a.m., Nov. 6, 1977, the dam above Toccoa Falls College burst, sending 176 million gallons of water raging through the sleeping campus and taking 39 lives. The story behind the headlines. A dramatic account of Christian victory in the face of tragedy. Introduction by Rosalynn Carter. 160 pages, trade paper, $2.95.

CRIMINAL FOREVER, by Gary Ziehl as told to Merribeth E. Olson. Gary Ziehl was an habitual criminal for whom no hope was held. But for fear of the hangman's noose he might have killed. But since his dramatic conversion, the law's somber prophecy that he would be a criminal forever has been proven wholly untrue. 96 pages, paper, $1.95.

FIBBER'S FABLES by Richard H. Boytim. The time-honored fables of Aesop retold in a bright, new format. Complete with biblical applications. Great for kids! 96 pages, $1.75.

DARE TO SHARE by Marney Patterson. Sub-titled "Communicating the Good News" this is an encouraging handbook on relating the Christian faith to others. Affirms that God's Word does not return void and those sharing it (whether from person to person or from the pulpit) should expect results. 122 pages, paper, $1.95

EVOLUTION: ITS COLLAPSE IN VIEW? by Henry Hiebert examines the teaching of evolution and finds several crucial areas in which the famous theory simply cannot face the facts of modern science. 171 pages, paper, $2.50.

THE BUSHMAN AND THE SPIRITS by Barney Lacendre as told to Owen Salway is the fascinating life story of a former Indian witch doctor, his conversion to Christ, his experiences with witchcraft, and his ministry for the Lord. 185 pages, paper, $2.95.